Living Wild
and Domestic

Living Wild
and Domestic

The Education of

a Hunter-Gardener

Robert Kimber

THE LYONS PRESS

Guilford, Connecticut
An Imprint of The Globe Pequot Press

The Lyons Press is an imprint of The Globe Pequot Press.

Printed in the United States of America

10 9 8 7 6 5 4 3 2 1

Design by Claire Zoghb

The Library of Congress Cataloging-in-Publication Data is available on file.

ISBN 1-58574-684-3

For Alexandra and Garrett Conover

best friends of the trail and the hunt,
keepers of the philosophers' tent

CONTENTS

PREFACE AND ACKNOWLEDGMENTS | XI

PROLOGUE:
PORCUPINE STEW AND ASPARAGUS | 1

I. KID STUFF | 13

II. GROWING UP CONFUSED | 37

III. VENTURES IN THE STOCK MARKET | 57

IV. DISH-FED RETAINERS | 85

V. CONTEXT NORTH: HUNTING
ALL THE TIME | 105

VI. FOOD, SPORT, AND WILD HUSBANDRY | 143

EPILOGUE:
ASPARAGUS REVISITED | 183

NOTES | 193

VENATOR. On my word, master, this is a gallant
          Trout; what shall we do with him?
PISCATOR. Marry, e'en eat him to supper. . . .

IZAAK WALTON, *The Compleat Angler*

PREFACE AND ACKNOWLEDGMENTS

A couple of years ago I sat down to write what I thought would be a fairly short essay exploring the perhaps irrational but nonetheless powerful love I felt for my dog. Many months and interruptions later, I'd written a short book that ranged far beyond that original vague conception and into reflections on animals wild and domestic, on creatures of the forest, pasture, and hearth, on the hunt and the garden.

Wherever else those reflections took me, they almost all seemed linked in one way or another to a couple of basic human questions: What do we eat, and how do we acquire what we eat? And because those questions bear directly on how much land we leave wild, how much we put to the plow, and how much we pave over, our answers to them reflect our vision of the creation and of right living in it. ". . . [O]ne of the great dreams of man," Barry Lopez has written, "must be to find some place between the extremes of nature and civilization where it is possible to live without regret." This book is a partial chronicle of my own search for that moral and physical place. Finding it has to remain a dream, of course. There is no escaping regret.

But unattainable as that place may be, the search for it has been far from gloomy or disheartening. On the contrary, it's been an exhilarating journey, made so largely because of the many good people who have been my companions on it. I can't possibly thank any of them enough, but I'll try. Thanks first to my wife, Rita, the master gardener to whom I am a mere apprentice and who has always understood that finding and growing food on the turf where one lives is one of the most worthwhile things a citizen of this planet can do. And thanks to our son, Greg, who has learned that lesson well, along with the practical skills attendant to it, and has taken it with him into his adult life. Nor can I forget our dog Lucy here, that bright animal spirit whose presence in our lives started me writing these pages but who is, sadly, no longer with us as this book goes to print.

With my old friend, Don Yeaton, thirty-five years my senior and gone now too, I shared the joys of eating deer meat for the best part of two winters; and in the last couple of decades, it has been my privilege to go afield with many skillful, thoughtful, and respectful hunters, fishers, and travelers of the bush from Vermont, Quebec, Ontario, Labrador, and Maine. I won't begin to name all the names for fear of leaving some out; but to Jerry Stelmok and to Alexandra and Garrett Conover, to whom this book is dedicated, I owe special thanks for our times together in the woods and for many hours of good talk about the issues at the heart of this book.

Beyond the circle of personal friends, I am much indebted to many writers, both living and dead, who have explored these same fields before me. High on that list is Richard Nelson, whose work is cited frequently in these pages. As anthropologist and participant, he has written eloquently and thoughtfully about hunting and foraging; in his book *Heart and Blood: Living with Deer in America*, he has studied issues of wildlife management with great thoroughness and fairness. My thanks also go to my Maine neighbor Bernd Heinrich; to Ted Kerasote, Barry Lopez, Paul Shepard, and Wallace Stegner; to poets Hayden Carruth, John Haines, and Mary Oliver. I'm grateful not just for specific passages cited here but for the entire bodies of their works. Wendell Berry's writings, too, have been particularly formative of my thinking about land, animals, food, and community. And then there is Aldo Leopold. Who has ever made clearer how indispensable the wild is to the domestic, how "land yields a cultural harvest"?

To protect the privacy of some individuals mentioned here, I have changed names and identifying details.

For reading this book or parts of it in manuscript form, I thank Rita, Greg, Jerry, Garrett, Alexandra, Dean and Sheila Bennett, Wes McNair, Neil McDonald, Susan Shetterly, and Taylor Stoehr. The book is the better for their many useful suggestions. Whatever factual errors, misinterpretations, or failures of judgment remain are entirely mine.

PROLOGUE:
PORCUPINE STEW
AND ASPARAGUS

Lucy's sharp, yipping bark means she has come upon another creature, whether chickadee, red squirrel, chipmunk, or moose. I look up from filing the chain saw on the back porch to see her dancing wildly around a slow, waddling beast heading unperturbed toward our abandoned sheep shed. Grateful that I'm on hand to intervene, I call the dog off. She will be spared a nose- and mouthful of quills; I will be spared the expense and inconvenience of another trip to the vet's office, where a porcupine encounter sent us only two days ago.

I pick up my .22 and go down to the sheep shed, which now serves as a catchall for lumber, fence posts, a johnboat. The porcupine has sought refuge in a corner behind a roll of snow fencing, and when I pull the roll away, the animal assumes its defensive posture, head tucked into the corner, rear end toward me, quills fanned out like a peacock's tail feathers. I shoot it in the back of the head; it slumps to the floor, killed instantly; not a muscle or a nerve so much as twitches. But just to make sure, I check with a stick from the lumber pile. I don't want quills in my hands and arms any more than I want them in Lucy's nose. The animal does not stir as the soft pine stick gathers a pompom of quills from its back.

When I pick the porcupine up by its left hind foot, the long guard hairs of its lower leg are soft in my hand. I carry the animal outside and lay it belly-up on the grass under a lilac bush. A dead porcupine on its back is a vastly different prospect than a live one on its feet, quills erect and tail thrashing. If ever there was a soft underbelly, a porcupine's is it, a vulnerable expanse of paunch, this one covered now after the spring molt with only gray, wispy hair that barely veils the skin underneath.

The first cut I attempt tells me my pocketknife is dull, and I go up to the house to hone it. Surely, I think as I work with the whetstone, I had two legitimate reasons for shooting this porcupine. Preventing a dog–porcupine face-off may have been my first consideration, but then porcupine enjoys a well-deserved reputation as a bush delicacy. It has been compared with lamb, but that comparison is ridiculous. The glory of all wild meat is that it does not taste like any domestic meat. Young porcupine is sweet, tender, delicate, and tastes like young porcupine, like nothing else. And if all the children, myself included, who grew up detesting liver for the tough, stringy, leathery, murky-tasting stuff that store-bought liver usually is had ever tasted porcupine liver, they would detest no more.

So I can justify my action on two counts: protection of

my domestic animal and hence of my economic interests (an agriculturalist's reason) and the acquisition of food (a hunter's reason). But will either of those arguments stand up to even a cursory moral critique, or am I just rationalizing what was at bottom the needless killing of a fellow creature?

My wife would argue later that I should have let the porcupine get away. Lucy's run-in with a porcupine two days ago did not make another inevitable. "If he'd stayed around," Rita said, "we could have taught Lucy to leave him alone. There he was, minding his own business, just trying to make an honest living, and look what it got him."

However skeptical I may feel about teaching a dog to leave a porcupine alone, I had to admit that I had sacrificed a wild animal to save myself possible expense and inconvenience. I've always proclaimed the priority of the wild animal over the domestic and condemned the destruction of wolves, cougars, and prairie dogs to make way for sheep and cattle. Consistency would seem to require that I shoot the dog, not the porcupine. My dog is a pet, a luxury; she contributes nothing tangible to human welfare. The stockman can at least argue that the loss of even one beef animal means not only economic loss for him but also the loss of food for others. I had killed a wild animal on the mere possibility, not the certainty, that it might cause my dog some pain and me some minor expense.

Well, all right. Chalk that one up against me. But surely the food argument is incontrovertible. If I kill an animal and eat it, I'm not dealing in maybes or possibilities. Meat on the table is meat on the table. Killing for food is not killing to protect any questionable economic interests that probably would have gotten along quite nicely without protection anyhow.

Razor-sharp knife in hand, I head back to my skinning job. I cut around wrists and ankles, slit down the insides of the legs to the midline of the belly, cut down the midline from throat to anus. As I start to peel the hide back from legs and belly, Rita, who has been shopping in town, returns home and comes to see what I'm doing. That she will disapprove is a given, but there will be no harsh words. We are each too acutely aware of our own confusions, inconsistencies, and irrationalities to come down too hard on the other.

"Poor baby," she says, "look at the little hands and feet."

Her remark is not sentimental. She is not out to add Porky the Porcupine to the Disney pantheon of Bambi the Deer and Thumper the Rabbit. She is just acknowledging a kinship that the appearance of the animal's limbs instantly suggests. Despite the long claws and the pebbly skin, the feet with their five toes and naked soles look remarkably human, and even though the hands, which the porcupine does in fact use in handlike fashion for food gathering, have only four digits, their similarity to our hands is striking.

Decry this as blatant, unscientific anthropomorphizing if you will, but the human impulse to see ourselves in animals and animals in us, to talk with them, cohabit with them, be suckled and reared by them—all this from Leda and the swan to Romulus and Remus to Mowgli–testifies to a dream citizenship in a world where no sharp lines are drawn between gods, men, and animals. For hunting cultures, kinship with animals is a fact reflected in their totemism and mythology.

In the cosmology of the Koyukon people in Alaska, it was the Great Raven who created the earth, its plants and animals, and its human beings. In the Distant Time, animals and humans were the same. They shared a common language, and animals can still understand human speech today. The Koyukon may address an animal directly, pleading for its blessing and protection, and they are careful not to say things or behave in ways that will offend the animal. For them, not to anthropomorphize (and not to recognize that animals zoomorphize) would be a sign of colossal ignorance, willful denial of our common ancestry and shared life in the present. When Rita kneels next to a dead porcupine and says, "Poor baby," she is acknowledging that clanship, our common origins in the same mix of clay and breath.

The Cartesian proscription against anthropomorphizing has always seemed to me both obtuse and arrogant, a kind of professional prissiness some scientists adopt to set themselves apart from the ignorant masses who, on seeing a dog bounce up and down wagging his tail, venture to say the dog is "happy." But for the observer or scientist who recognizes a kinship with animals, the prohibition on anthropomorphizing is rooted in a humility that acknowledges the creature's otherness, all those ways in which human and porcupine are not alike and that constitute, perhaps even more than its kinship with us, the animal's mystery and sacredness. If we see only ourselves in animals, we will never see *them*. To anthropomorphize in that way is to sentimentalize and invent for white-tailed deer a domestic life that any 1950s family in Greenwich, Connecticut, would have been proud of.

Rita goes up to the house to put away the groceries; I finish dressing out the porcupine. I cut the tail free, put my foot on it, and lift the animal by its hind feet, peeling the skin away right up to the back of the skull, where I cut the head off. I open the body cavity, pull out a loop of lower intestine near the anus, cut it, and strip out the feces. I cut the esophagus free where it comes through the diaphragm and pull out the liver, kidneys, intestines. You don't have to have vast experience in comparative anatomy to realize that evolution has allotted most of the space inside a porcupine to its digestive system, which makes up one-quarter of the animal's body weight. A porcupine is a kind of mammalian pear or crookneck squash, its lower bulge filled with its long, labyrinthian guts, its proportionately tiny heart and lungs tucked in as an afterthought way up inside the neck.

Because the porcupine is not a long-distance runner, pulmonary and cardiovascular capacity is not a high priority. Far more important is the ability to convert bark and leaves into energy. Because those mainstays of the porcupine's diet number among nature's more intractable foodstuffs, evolution has seen to it that the porcupine has a physical plant that can break them down. In the caecum, a sac about the size of the stomach but located where the small and large intestines meet, bacterial enzymes accomplish what mammalian digestive enzymes cannot. But because the enzymes work slowly, the digestive process is also slow and the digestive tract long to allow for absorption of nutrients.

I am acutely aware of the genius of this animal as I dismember him, handling the pearly, undulating beauty of his guts, the red glow of his muscle, the still-present heat of this life I have ended. Even our most intricate human inventions seem clumsy and lumbering compared with the perfection of this modest beast, a perfection of mind and spirit as well as of body. In his many years of studying porcupines in the Catskills, Uldis Roze found that the animal was

a hunter of leaves. Unlike the grazing ruminants of the plains that crop a field of grass and find any number of species acceptable fodder, the porcupine must hunt its food by discovering the rare trees in the forest that will best sustain it. Out of a thousand forest trees in the Catskills, one or two are acceptable lindens and one is a big-tooth aspen. To locate and return to those trees, the porcupine uses all the skills of the hunter: memory, attention to landmark and local detail, persistence. That explains why the American psychologist L. W. Sackett (1913) found that the North American porcupine has an extraordinary ability to learn complex mazes and to remember them as much as a hundred days afterward.

Would Descartes have said, "The porcupine thinks; therefore, it is"? I doubt it, but I would hardly call Uldis Roze less a scientist because he uses words like *memory* and *attention, learn* and *remember,* to describe the porcupine's capabilities and behavior. I take at face value the remark a Koyukon elder made repeatedly to anthropologist Richard Nelson: "Every animal knows way more than you do."

The porcupine is skinned and dressed out now. No edible scrap of him will go to waste. At the outdoor faucet I rinse off the body, the heart, liver, kidneys. The skin, quills, feet, intestines, and bladder I will give an honorable burial. A pre-industrial hunter might have dyed the quills and decorated belts, clothing, moccasins, and pouches with them. Dried and mounted on a wooden handle, Uldis Roze says, the bristly underside of the tail that aids the porcupine in climbing trees makes an excellent comb. The long, curved claws that let the porcupine cling to fissures in rough bark I could make into a necklace or bracelet, but I will make neither. I live, after all, in a different economy, and I ask my porcupine's forgiveness for my yielding to other imperatives and for my failure of piety.

As I cut the animal up into stew-sized pieces in our well-stocked kitchen, I have to concede, too, that in the context of that same economy, my hunter's justification for this kill may not stand up either. We do not *need* this animal for food. We have plenty else to live on. We have storage tins full of rice and beans; we have little plastic tubs full of tofu in the fridge; we have dried bananas from Nicaragua and dried apricots from Turkey.

Given the ready availability of vegetable foods, one could easily argue that I killed this porcupine simply for a taste treat, merely to satisfy a trivial whim. One could argue that society's ability to grow adequate amounts of nourishing vegetarian fare makes the killing of any animal for food unnecessary. And if we add to that the darker side of growing vegetable crops by modern large-scale agricultural methods, a prohibition on killing animals would seem all the more urgent. Just consider how many animal deaths each cupful of granola represents. How many nesting trees were felled to clear the fields to grow the oats, peanuts, and sunflower seeds? How many buffalo died to make way for the wheat and cornfields of Kansas and Nebraska? How many raccoons, rabbits, squirrels, skunks, and porcupines have the trucks that cart the oats, peanuts, and sunflower seeds pulverized on our highways and byways? How many square miles of Alaskan wildlife habitat have been and will be destroyed to drill the oil wells that will keep our trucks and tractors rolling? With so many surrogate killers doing in animals to keep me in innocent, bloodless food, how dare I take the life of one more creature? The global network of industrial agriculture tells me I dare not. Hunting, the whole inexorable drift of our world tells me, is obsolete, passé. Hunting is nostalgic playacting.

If I pursue this line of thought much farther, I'll soon be utterly depressed and dispirited. So I don't. "Lighten up, man," I tell myself. "Give yourself a break. Nobody's expecting categorical imperatives from you. Make a little sense of your life on your own turf and you'll be doing just fine."

In the course of the following week, during which our porcupine provides us with four superb evening meals— liver one night, porcupine stew for the other three, all with fresh asparagus from the garden on the side—I do lighten up considerably.

So does Rita. As we are sopping up the last of the gravy and sucking the last of the bones clean, she says to me, "You know, if porcupine were a vegetable, I'd grow it."

"And if asparagus were an animal," I say, "I'd shoot it."

Living Wild
and Domestic

I.

KID STUFF

I've kept animals most of my life and killed animals most of my life. I've killed many I've kept and killed many more I haven't kept. I've feasted on fish, flesh, and fowl, wild and domestic: fish pulled out of rivers and lakes with fly rods, spinning rods, bait-casting rods; fish hauled up on a string through holes in two and three feet of ice; chickens and ducks beheaded with an ax; squirrels shot out of tree-tops; cottontails shot in the hedgerows of farm fields; partridge and deer shot in the warmth and color of New England Indian summers; ptarmigan and caribou shot in subarctic cold and snow; sheep and pigs and beef cattle poleaxed and bled and dismembered in my own or a neighbor's dooryard.

The trail of blood I've spilled with my own hands is long and wide; the trail is even longer and wider if you count the blood anonymous killers have shed to bring me Christmas turkeys via the Shop 'n Save meat department, escargots and filet mignon via the immaculately white tablecloth in the Restaurant de Paris.

The first creatures I killed were cold-blooded, but there was nothing cold-blooded, nothing premeditated or calculated, about my killing them. Just the opposite. I was so young when I started fishing that I can't begin to remember how young I was. I was all blood—hot blood—and no brain. The pale cast of thought was the farthest thing from whatever mind I had. In one of the few family photographs still left from my preschool years, I'm in a rowboat with my brother and my father, holding a fishing rod. I probably started fishing as soon as I was steady enough on my feet to walk to the water. Learning to walk, learning to talk, learning to fish all go back beyond the reach of my memory. I learned to fish long before I even thought about thinking.

Among the many debts of gratitude I owe my father, one is for choosing a place on water to raise his two boys. All I had to do to go fishing any day after school or any day during the summer vacation was step out our door and walk the hundred or so yards to the modest little lake across the road from our house in suburban New Jersey. There, practically on my doorstep, with garden worms or strips of bacon or gobs of spongy, pasty Wonder Bread packed onto my hook, I could catch bluegills, sunnies, and yellow perch hand over fist. That I killed them hand over fist, that I inflicted pain on them in catching them, that I inflicted pain on the worms I impaled on my hooks, none of that occurred to me. Despite the technology of rod, line, and hook I used, I was still a natural predator, as thoughtless about catching, killing, and eating fish as any osprey, otter, or kingfisher. The lives and deaths of those fish fit so seamlessly into my life that their deaths did not register as deaths at all. I inhaled; I exhaled. I killed fish; I ate fish.

In those earliest years of my killing life, I was as close to being an animal among animals as I can ever remember being, one more predator using his (minimal) knowledge and skills to find and kill his prey. I would not have starved or even missed one of my three squares a day had I never caught a fish in my young life. But even if my fishing was not a matter of life and death, we ate everything I caught, though when I went racing out of the house with rod and a few slices of stale Wonder Bread in hand, I was not thinking about food; I was thinking about fun. I liked fishing. I liked the maybeness of it. Maybe a fish would bite and maybe it wouldn't. Panfish, bless them, bite often enough and eagerly enough that "maybe" had a comforting element of certainty about it. Maybe not on this cast or the next or the next, but surely on one of them. I just didn't know which one. I didn't fish to live, though fishing made up, in a small way, part of my family's living; and I didn't live to fish, though living, as I had come to understand life in the few years I had lived, would have been a drab and dreary business without fishing, drained of color, adventure.

The word *sport* may have entered my vocabulary by then, but only as an abstraction. If fishing had been a sport, it would have been recreation, a hobby, a pastime, diversion. I didn't pass time fishing; I stopped time; I made it stand still. I filled it so full that it overflowed, time without end. I wasn't diverted, I was focused, intent. Fishing was not recreation but creation, the finding and making of a self in the world, learning the world, feeding the self. I was not recreating because I had not been destroyed or diminished. I was still too young and dumb to know that school was work and fishing was play. I had not yet learned division, long or short. Fractions were beyond me. I caught; I killed; I ate. To fish was to be both utterly calm and utterly frenzied, utterly oblivious and utterly attentive, to attain a state of consciousness in which consciousness disappeared. If the word *fun* can even begin to encompass that experience, then that's the kind of fun fishing was. And still is.

❧

Jump ahead a few years. I'm ten or eleven. I find in the cellar a rusted, octagonal-barreled, single-shot .22 rifle, Remington Arms Co., not a bolt action but a rolling breechblock.

Remember, I'm ten or eleven by now, old enough to be corrupted, and I am. I've been reading Fenimore Cooper and Zane Gray. I've seen the evil Magua finally fall to Hawkeye's unerring aim with Killdeer, seen Lew Wetzel rescue fair Nell from the filthy clutches of renegade Jim Girty in *The Spirit of the Border*.

All right. So maybe this rusty little rifle didn't really go back to Natty Bumpo, but that rolling block, that octagonal barrel bespoke a frontier lineage. I wanted to think my Remington single shot was a closer relative to Killdeer than it was to any M1 Garand or even a Springfield or Enfield. It had been my father's boyhood gun, and my father had seen Buffalo Bill in Madison Square Garden. My father was Buffalo Bill's contemporary. So was my father's .22. Didn't that count for something?

This rifle oozed romance. I would resurrect it from rust. I scrubbed its barrel and receiver endlessly with steel wool and 3-in-1 oil. I ran patch after patch after patch soaked with Hoppe's No. 9 through its corroded bore. I stripped and sanded its walnut stock and forend, rubbed in linseed oil and rubbed and rubbed some more until the wood glowed with a soft sheen. I restored the little rifle to glory. It would sing Killdeer's song of swift death again.

My father catechized me in firearm safety. What's the first thing you do when you pick up a gun, any gun? You keep the muzzle pointed at the ground and you open the action to make sure the gun isn't loaded. What do you never do with a gun? You never, no, never ever point a gun, not a real gun, not a toy gun, not any gun, no, never, never do you point any gun at anyone, not on purpose, not out of carelessness, no, never, never, never. I learned so well that water-pistol shootouts still leave me feeling a bit uneasy.

My father didn't have to teach me how to shoot. There isn't, after all, a whole lot to be taught. You line up the sights, exhale, hold your breath for the fraction of a second it takes to squeeze off the shot. I'd been practicing this routine for years with toy guns while my issues of *Outdoor Life* and *Field & Stream* piled up and I daydreamed of joining gun editor Jack O'Conner on hunts for bighorn sheep in the Rockies, for brown bears in Alaska. After years of mock shooting, the real thing came easily. Now, with a bullet-shooting rifle in my hands at last, I found it a cinch to chew the bull's-eye out of a smallbore target. I could set up a row of tin cans and send them tumbling, one shot, one can. Who needed more than a single shot if he knew how to hit what he aimed at? Natty Bumpo didn't need more than a single shot when he finally picked Magua off the top of that cliff. "The surrounding rocks themselves were not steadier than the piece became, for the single instant that it poured out its contents."

Oh, yes, yes. In the wilds of the gravel pit where I went to burn up box after box of BB caps, out there in the Great Beyond beyond the Delaware, Lackawanna, & Western railroad tracks and beyond the double concrete lanes of Route 6, out there the muzzle of my piece too rivaled the rocks for steadiness, and with each tin can that fell the noble Uncas was avenged; avenged too was the spirited, raven-haired Cora who had flung these last words in the face of her foul captor: "Kill me if thou wilt, detestable Huron; I will go no further." Then down she went in the muddled melee, a savage's blade sheathed in her flawless white bosom.

I quickly learned, though, that our New Jersey commuters' town only thirty miles due west of New York City placed serious limitations on the skills of an accomplished rifleman. The French and Indian Wars were over. Laws dictated when you could hunt for what and when you couldn't, and for most of the year, you couldn't hunt for much. Another law (eminently sensible in that densely populated little state) forbid hunting with any kind of rifle. Still another law forbid anyone under the age of sixteen, I believe it was, to hunt unless accompanied by an adult.

Had my father been as keen a hunter as he was a fisherman, he might have gotten me a .410 and taken me afield every fall as religiously as he took me to ponds and rivers every spring. But for whatever reasons, his heart just wasn't in hunting; if I was going to hunt before I was sixteen, I would have to figure out the how and where and when myself.

What kind of game was available in that tightly controlled little world for an underage, illegal hunter whose favored (and only) weapon was as illegal as he was?

Rats were available. Dick Hardy, one of my father's fishing buddies and so, by extension, one of my fishing buddies, lived on the edge of Mountain Lakes, not quite in it. His place was off the Eastside Road, which marked the outermost limits of inhabited Mountain Lakes. Also, Dick's place was, by suburban standards, big, an acre and a half, two acres maybe; and the back of it backed on woods, and what the woods backed on, I don't remember. Dick's neighbors on either side were at a comfortable remove from him, comfortable enough that he could keep animals, modest-sized ones anyhow. He had hutches full of rabbits and a large chicken run so pounded and picked over by the feet and beaks of chickens that not a wisp of green grew anywhere on it. And underneath that chicken run must have been a maze, a labyrinth of rat burrows; the cementlike surface of the run was pockmarked with rat holes. The traffic in and out of those holes was heavy. Dick resented feeding his mash and cracked corn to rats, and he engaged my friend John Miller and me to reduce the rat population, a nickel a head.

In the late afternoons of those years, several fifteen-minute adventure serials came on the radio: *Superman* ("It's a bird; it's a plane. No! It's Superman!"), *Jack Armstrong* ("Jack Armstrong, *Jack Armstrong*, JACK ARMSTRONG! The All-American Boy!") and *Blackhawk* ("Hawkaaaa!"). Among them was *Tennessee Jed*, each episode of which began with a rifle shot ringing out (Ptschinnnggg!) and Tennessee's companion complimenting him on his marksmanship: "Got 'im, Tennessee, dead center."

And so, when John and I clambered up onto the low roof of Dick's chicken coop and waited, never very long, for rats to appear, then took turns potting them, John would turn to me or I to him as each rat bit the dust and say, with head tilted back and eyes squinted down to steely little slits, "Got 'im, Tennessee, dead center."

But how could any kid whose images of hunting and hunters had been formed by Leatherstocking romances and elk hunts reported in *Outdoor Life* yet whose first reality afield was nickel-a-head bounty hunting for Norway rats, how could such a kid have anything but ambivalent feelings about hunting? Even a psychically robust, unsentimental eleven-year-old boy is bound to see himself as an ignoble and somewhat grubby figure as he picks up a dozen or more rats by their scaly tails at the end of a summer afternoon and tosses the carcasses into the woods back of Dick's place. All our Tennessee-Jed posing to the contrary, rats were still rats.

Killing rats was, of course, a socially useful and socially sanctioned thing to do. Rats are vermin of the vilest sort, destructive, prolific, disease-ridden; but my social usefulness, the contribution I was making to the health of Dick's chicken yard and pocketbook, in no way compensated me for my tarnished self-image. Robert the Ratter was not a title I wanted to see emblazoned on my coat of arms. Shooting rats in a chicken coop may not be the exact equivalent of shooting fish in a barrel, but it's close enough that I never went to school the next day and told the guys how many rats I'd shot the day before.

Other uses of .22 rifles were not sanctioned. Just about anything else John and I did with our guns—except for plinking in the gravel pit—could get us into trouble. Whenever I snuck the rifle out of the house and made off into the woods that skirted our town on the west, I was always looking over my shoulder, always worried that the eye of the law might spot me, the iron hand of the law clamp down on my shoulder.

Just as bad, if not worse, was the iron hand of conscience. Simply being out in the woods with gun in hand was crime enough; actually shooting it compounded that crime. No target, not even something as safe and inanimate as a knot in a rotting stump, was legitimate. Things animate harbored endless dangers. The flap on the cartridge box said, "Range, one mile. *Be Careful!*" Where might a bullet that missed a gray squirrel high in an oak tree land? Not having killed the squirrel, the bullet would surely fly up and up until, its energy expended, it began its plunge to earth. And who or what would be below it as it plummeted down? Would Mrs. Brighton, our fourth-grade teacher, short, squat, square, sturdy, be found sprawled in her driveway that afternoon, a tiny hole punched through her graying brown hair, her car door still open, her groceries spilling out of her paper bags where she fell, the neighbors' dog tearing at the pork chops she had been planning to cook for dinner that night? What might we kill if we failed to kill what we meant to kill?

I had learned my lessons in firearm safety well. I knew that within a mile of anywhere I stood, even if I was in the woods that separated our town from the truck farms and the golf course in Rockaway valley, there were houses, people, cars, dogs. Unless I could see the backstop that would catch my bullet, I would content myself with aiming an empty rifle and saying, "Bang."

But there were backstops, and I did fire live rounds, usually at dead branches, at rocks, at anything that would register a hit. Other targets presented themselves as well. Unlike squirrels, painted turtles did not inhabit treetops. Turtles sunned themselves on sodden logs on the shores of Birchwood Lake, and the shore rose up in a solid, dependable backstop behind them. No danger there. Unless we paddled too close to them in our leaky, cracked-ribbed old canoe, the turtles would bask immobile in the summer sun. They sat better than sitting ducks, and because they had no fur or feathers but looked more like rocks from a distance, mere humps of something solid, shooting them seemed somehow permissible. They were tempting targets; but gun-crazy kid though I may have been, I had enough moral imagination even then to resist that temptation.

Often enough in my boyhood ramblings I had seen these turtles and often held them in my hands. Up close, a painted turtle was no mere bump on a log. Its finely articulated shell made it appear not crude, lumpish, gross. It was not of an order so far beneath higher forms of life, beneath sparrows and chipmunks even, and so far beneath *me* that I could take its life on a whim and get away scot-free. No, on the contrary. If I had ever thought the non-mammalian, rocklike armor of this creature could somehow protect me and absolve me from the guilt of inflicting a stupid, gratuitous death on it, I couldn't have been more deluded. Its shell was not armor at all but every bit as fragile as the pale blue fragments of a pipped robin's egg.

In retrospect, I realize that those inhibitions I felt about killing a turtle represented a step forward in my religious education. But if anyone had asked me then why I had chosen not to commit turtle murder, I probably would have said shooting a turtle on a log was not sporting. Sport was, by this time, assuming an increasingly important place in my life, not so much sport as recreation but sport as an ethical code. Had I in fact taken up turtle killing, failure in sportsmanship would have been the least of my crimes, a venial footnote appended to a deadly sin; but if I had been asked at the time to explain what would be reprehensible about such an act, I probably would have seized on violation of the sporting ethic, which dictated what creatures one was allowed to kill and how one could kill them. Education in the sporting ethic, like any educational process, takes time and proceeds through stages of ever greater refinement. Central to sportsmanship, whether in football, tennis, hunting, or fishing, is fair play; and central to the idea of fair play is that we engage only worthy adversaries.

I knew a painted turtle placidly sunning itself on a log was not a worthy adversary for a kid with a .22 rifle. My days of innocence were over. The predatory pleasure of catching panfish no longer satisfied. The pages of *Outdoor Life* and *Field & Stream* had shown me that the world offered far worthier prey. So had my father, on a much more modest level. He was no Ray Bergman, the great fishing guru of those years. He didn't travel west to fish the Snake, the Yellowstone, and the Madison. He never caught steelheads on Oregon's Umpqua. He didn't even travel north into the Catskills to fish the Beaverkill or the Esopus. But he shared at least some territory with Ray Bergman. He went on fishing trips to Maine. He caught big brookies there, landlocked salmon, togue. He spoke knowingly of the Kennebago River, the Parmacheenee Club. In our home territory, he fished the Flat Brook, the Musconetcong. On April 15, opening day of trout season in New Jersey, he left the house before daylight and met Carl Wrede at the Powerville Dam on the Rockaway River in Boonton. There, amid an army of other fishermen, he soon caught his limit of hatchery trout. He owned waders, a wicker creel, a fishing vest full of pockets, a beautiful little split-bamboo rod only seven and a half feet long but with enough backbone and authority to reach any lie my father wanted to reach on New Jersey's little suburban rivers.

Even before the Remington single shot, the rat killing, my reflections on turtles, I had started to evolve out of my fish-catching, fish-eating innocence. I could see the fish my father brought home from the Rockaway, the same kind of fish (though not so large by pounds and inches) that graced the magazine covers. Though still too young to wade trout streams and be entrusted with the fragile beauty of split bamboo, I was sopping up the lore and the mythology. It was perfectly obvious to me that my father's fish and the magazine-cover fish were fish of a higher order than my fish. Trout were sleek and streamlined and mottled with spots. They had no spiny dorsal fins to stick you with and no big, gobby, inedible scales you had to scrape off before you fried them. They needed the cool, moving waters of rivers to survive. Trout were noble and, being noble, had to live in noble surroundings and eat noble food: stoneflies, mayflies, caddisflies. They would not dream of eating Wonder Bread. Perch and bluegills, on the other hand, thrived in the warm, shallow, alga-infested waters of New Jersey's artificial lakes. If they would eat Wonder Bread, they would eat just about anything. They were not noble.

My father's fly rod too was of a vastly higher order than the stubby little metal rod or the bamboo poles I used to toss out my bobber and gob of worms. The differences were not just ones of physical beauty, vast as those differences were. How could even the most undiscriminating eye fail to see that a split-bamboo fly rod was to a bamboo pole what *Homo sapiens* was to *Homo erectus*, a highly evolved descendant from a gross, gangling ancestor? The only other role I had seen bamboo poles play, aside from serving as crude fishing rods, was as cores for transporting and storing rolled rugs. The very idea of my father's three-ounce rod with a rug rolled around it was more than absurd. The beauty of that rod went beyond functional simplicity—functional and simple as it was—into a territory I can only call exquisite: the walnut reel seat, the sleek lines of the cork grip, the silver lock ring with its minutely knurled rims, the tiny ring of the hook keeper, the translucent red agate in the stripper guide. So fine, elegant, and ancient did these things appear to my eye that I could imagine them coming from the tombs of the Pharaohs. The lock ring was perhaps a trifle large, but it was surely beautiful enough to have graced Nefertiti's finger. Gemlike, too, was the finish, that layer of varnish that glowed softly and transformed the maroon and yellow silk windings into rings of ruby and opal, and encased under that layer of varnish as if under the glass of a jeweler's showcase were the signatures of Abbey and Imbrie. Those names always made me think of Abbott and Costello, but of course I never let that thought find words. Abbey and Imbrie, Abercrombie and Fitch, Abercrombie's Camps, none of those names was taken in vain in our household. (I have since discovered that Abbey and Imbrie were not classy rod makers at all and that the rod I worshiped in my boyhood was probably one of many mass-produced rods sold under the Abbey and Imbrie label. What I did not know did not hurt me.)

But more important than all of these things was the rod's hexagonal delicacy, slender enough in the butt section but then tapering away almost into thin air in a tip scarcely larger in diameter than the line it carried. Now, fishing with a rod like that was *sporting*. A good-sized fish could break that wispy little tip. Fishing with a rod delicate enough that it could break made a worthy adversary of any fish three or four pounds and up, not that New Jersey's streams yielded many trout of that size, but the sheer theoretical breakability of the rod was in itself enough to satisfy the worthy-adversary requirement. In his second edition of *Trout* (1952), Ray Bergman notes, apropos of the then relatively new fiberglass rods and their near unbreakability, "A number of anglers resent the creation of anything unbreakable for fishing, on the grounds that it doesn't give the fish a fair chance. But of course one could easily handle that situation by never using a leader so strong that the fish can't break it."

Any decent, ethical human being would identify with those resentful anglers and justly condemn not the otherwise impeccably sporting Ray but his momentary lapse into sophistry here. A leader light enough to give the fish a sporting chance for escape is a gesture in the right direction but an insufficient one. The fisherman, after all, is out to kill the fish. (Please note that our discussion of sportsmanship here is taking place in the benighted 1950s, long before catch-and-release became standard practice in the sporting crowd.) Not many fishing situations give the fish the same opportunity. Pursuing white sharks with swim fins and a trident might; or going out to sea in a rowboat to hunt huge marlin, like Hemingway's old man. Giving a fish the chance to bust your leader is self-deception, just a sop to a bad conscience. Because even a record brook trout is highly unlikely to put even the most feeble fisherman's life at risk, the only halfway sporting thing the fisherman can do is to use a rod that the fish can destroy. If you're not going to let the fish have a shot at killing you, then the least you can do is give them a sporting chance to kill your rod, drive you off the river, and send you home with nothing but a handful of bamboo splinters to show for your pains.

Such, in any case, was the drift of my thinking as I

emerged from the dark ages of my unreflecting, meat-hunting childhood. Now that I had entered the moral universe of sport, hauling panfish out of the water with a bamboo pole would no longer do. Now that I understood the difference between sport and mere food gathering, my bamboo pole seemed crude as a caveman's club. It swung out over the water like a crane at a construction site, dipped down toward the surface, waited, rose again and swung back in toward shore with a tiny, wriggling burden dangling from it. No fish was too small to keep because no fish was too small to eat. But where was the sport, the fair play, in fishing like this? What chance did a tiny bluegill have against a pole that could pick up a rug? Equipped with this derrick I could probably even draw out leviathan with my hook.

No, there were bamboo poles, and there were bamboo fly rods; there was pithecanthropus, and there was Ray Bergman. It was time for me to begin my slow, step-by-step education in ever higher levels of sport. That meant, first, learning plug casting, tossing a five-eighth-ounce Jitterbug out sidearm with just enough thumb pressure on that wildly spinning reel to keep it from overrunning itself and building, in a second's time, a bird's nest so dense and tangled that the only solution was to cut it out and lose yards and yards of line. It meant fishing for pickerel and large-mouth bass, big game that added an element of maybe-not to the maybeness of fishing. They were nowhere near as plentiful as panfish, and standing on the grassy bank across from our house, tossing a Jitterbug or Pikie Minnow out into the cove there, I was not likely to catch one. But for now, learning was more important than catching. Learning how to control the lure, how to put it right where I wanted it, was like learning to shoot, a skill essential to the hunt. My father took me into the city to the Sportsman's Show, to that same Madison Square Garden where he had seen Buffalo Bill, and there I could watch the elite of the fishing world drop hookless lures into little floating target rings in a pool. My ambition was to get that good.

Once I'd advanced to the point where I could cast sidearm all evening with only an occasional backlash or two, I started casting overhand. The plug slammed down into the grass at my feet; it went flying up almost vertically into the air and came plummeting back down only a few yards in front of me in the water. But gradually, I made progress. The lure began to sail out in a gratifying arc. With a little more or less energy in the cast, a little more or less pressure on the spool of the reel, I developed increasing control over just how far the plug went. Soon I wasn't just practicing; I was fishing. On summer evenings after supper, my father and I would take the canoe out for a couple of hours on the lake. Now that I was skilled enough to drop my lure within a six-foot circle eight times out of ten, we could go to the coves where the bass and pickerel lurked. I could cast to pockets of open water in the rafts of lily pads, to tantalizing lies under overhanging trees, next to shoreline rocks and downed logs.

Sometimes I would overshoot and bounce the lure off a rock or, worse yet, heave it up into the brush on shore. Sometimes, while using a sinking lure, I would thumb badly and wind up with a dense tangle of line wound around the reel spool. The lure would sink to the bottom because I could not begin retrieving it right away, and once I had cleared the reel and begun the retrieve, the plug would hang up inextricably in a dense weed bed or lily-pad roots and I would lose it.

Making difficult casts, losing Dardevles on the bottom, getting skunked more often than not—all that contributed greatly to my sense of myself as a civilized human being, no mere meat hunter but a sportsman pursuing a worthy adversary. Unlike panfish that could practically be scooped out of the water with a bucket, bass and pickerel made themselves scarce; they hid in lairs only the skilled could find and penetrate. Unlike panfish that could only struggle weakly as they were hauled out of their element, bass could leap up out of the water and toss a fistful of treble hooks right back into a fisherman's face. Bass and pickerel were not the same kind of threat to my life that I was to theirs, but they could at least exact a figurative pound of flesh from me. I can't remember anymore what Jitterbugs and Flatfish and Hula Poppers cost fifty years ago, but I do remember that whatever money I earned mowing neighborhood lawns could easily disappear replacing lost lures.

The step up to plug casting, bass, and pickerel was progress. Stubby little-kid rods, bamboo poles, and Wonder Bread were things of the past, but there were still miles for me to go, and the next one involved hunting those same bass and pickerel with a fly rod. My mother, as a dutiful young wife of a bygone era, had done her best to understand just what it was my father found so fascinating about standing up to his middle in flowing water and offering fake food to fish that probably weren't even there. She had been equipped with an eight-and-a-half-foot rod, the standard wicker creel, a couple of boxes for wet and dry flies, and hip boots. She could hardly wait for her firstborn son to be old enough to take this stuff off her hands. Unfortunately, her firstborn showed no more enthusiasm for fishing than she had, so she had to wait another couple of years for me to come along, and even though she had gradually and tactfully made it clear to my father that she would not be hurt if he went fishing without her and even though her fishing gear had consequently not seen much action after the first few years of her marriage, she was still much relieved when she could put it all into my eager and waiting hands with complete assurance that it would never come back into her own.

Out my father and I went onto the front lawn, where, with rod, line, leader, and a fly with the hook snipped off it, I learned his style of casting: all in the wrist and forearm, lift that line up off the water before you begin your backcast; the rod tip moves between eleven and one o'clock; wait for the backcast loop to unroll, put the power on *smoothly*, let that line down *gently*, oh so gently, softly; you suspend it out there on your breath; that fly has to come down as if it had a parachute on it.

Casting a hookless fly on the lawn was all well and good, all part of the apprenticeship, but what I wanted was some real action. So it was back to the panfish, the only fish that would put up with a tyro, the only fish that would forgive me my flubbed casts and come swarming after any ragged wet fly I tossed out to them. Having caught two- and three-pound bass and pickerel on the plug-casting tackle, I felt some loss of status in going back to the panfish. It was a bit like being busted from corporal back to PFC, even though the demotion was self-imposed. But one compensation was getting the feel of real fish on that fine, delicate, yet tough wand of split Tonkin cane. Another was the perceptible progress, the getting better, lifting the line off the water smoothly and cleanly, not heaving it off in a horrendous rip and tear of water, the sweet curve of a tight loop uncoiling on a perfect backcast.

My mother's rod was on the soft side, a real buggy whip. What it lacked in power, I had to make up for in technique, and there were limits beyond which the rod could not go, even in hands more skilled than mine. It punished any sloppiness, every moment of inattention. So it forced me to become a reasonably competent caster. I worked at fly casting and fly fishing with a diligence and devotion and concentration I find impossible to bring to any work that is not essentially play. My sidekick John Miller did too. He worked and played, if anything, better than I did, certainly with more natural talent. A rangy, skinny, blond-haired kid whose total lack of body fat along with his prowess as a long-distance runner would later earn him the high school epithet "Legs of Wire," John was the endearing black sheep of his family. If he had been born in medieval England, he could have become a world-class poacher, skillful, wily, physically tough and indefatigable, and blessed with a big brown-eyed charm and guilelessness that probably could have gotten him off the hook even if the Sheriff of Nottingham had caught him paunching out a deer in Sherwood Forest. Son of a successful, hardworking insurance agent and the chairwoman of the Mountain Lakes Garden Club and PTA, younger brother to a handsomely blond sister and to a powerhouse of a brother one year his senior with gifts of great intelligence (astronomically high IQ, NROTC scholarship to Yale), athletic ability (star of football, basketball, and track teams), and masculine beauty (our high school English teacher breathlessly described him as a Greek god), John decided early in life that the competition was just too stiff, and he veered off the family high road to explore byways frequented by muskrats, tadpoles, and trout. I'm happy to say he has remained there all his life, and it is on those byways that we still meet, our old jokes and legends still intact and John still fishing with the same bamboo rod he bought in 1949.

When we had gotten good enough standing on the grass bank in front of my house, casting for panfish, we graduated to the canoe and went after bass and pickerel with poppers, deer-hair frogs, the whole instrumentarium of warm-water fly fishing. My buggy whip was far from ideal for handling those big, wind-resistant bass bugs, but it would have to do. It was the rod I had, and if I often cursed its lack of authority, its weak-kneed performance when I wanted to push out just a few more feet of line or buck a breeze, I could console myself with the thought that every obstacle I put in my own path made me that much more sporting, that much more ethical. And as John and I grew both in physical size and in fly-fishing skill, we were soon joining my father and Carl Wrede to fish the Rockaway for trout on opening day, to make weekend jaunts with them to the Flat Brook and the Musconetcong. And because we were still kids, we had the sweet eternity of summer vacations and afternoons after school at our disposal. In a week we could put in more time on the river than my unenviable grown-up father could cobble together in a month. We started catching up on our elders fast. We often had the Rockaway below Powerville Dam all to ourselves. We learned about nymphs, duns, and spinners, about Quill Gordons, Light Cahills, Fan-Winged Royal Coachmen. We started tying our own flies.

And of course we started looking down our snotty youthful noses at the worm fishermen and spin casters and even the fly fishermen whose casting was not quite up to snuff, dubbing them whocksplotters. *Whock* was for the sound a fly line makes when a poor ignorant sod attempts to cast it, trying to make up in power and speed what he lacks in skill, knowledge, finesse, and noblesse, not just one whock actually but a whole series—whockwhock-whockwhock—as his back- and forecasts whip and flail ineffectually at the air and finally dump a tangle of line and leader on his own head. And *splot* for the sound a shoddy backcast makes when the fly and leader slap the water behind the caster. Anyone who whocked would also splot, hence, whocksplotter.

We advanced into ever more ethereal, more transcendental realms of sportsmanship. We gave up bait fishing in any form and for any fish whatsoever. We didn't even own spinning rods, those idiot sticks that any raw novice could become proficient with in a couple of hours. Our plug-casting rods saw less and less action and were finally relegated to the back of the closet. We became fly fishermen and, before too long, where trout were concerned, dry-fly fishermen only, the purest of the pure. It was irritating to see my father and Carl Wrede, neither of whom scorned worms when worms worked, continue to catch fish in the cold, roily waters of opening day while we fished hard all day and went home with empty creels. But our rewards came not in the form of delicious pan-sized fish rolled in flour and fried in a pan but in knowing ourselves superior beings.

By the time we were in our early teens, we had put away childish things. We still enjoyed a panful of trout or a big bass baked in the oven, but if anyone had suggested to me that I fished or hunted for the sake of meat, I would have been deeply insulted and indignant. In my young sportsman's eyes, anyone who fished and hunted primarily to acquire food was a lower order of human being. Vastly lower still was anyone who killed and then wasted the body of the fish or animal killed. Though sport and the refined skills it called for may have become my focus, I would still be outraged if I found, say, half a dozen bluegills tossed up on shore and rotting in the sun. The sportsman's code demanded respectful use of any creature a sportsman killed.

Violations of the sportsman's code were to be condemned, but the code itself was beyond question. It did not occur to me at that point in my life that designating certain creatures as "game" implied a set of highly dubious assumptions. We play games for amusement. To overstate the case a bit: Is it the brook trout's divine purpose to provide us with amusement? By what authority can we make sport of these creatures' lives? By what authority can we make them our playthings?

Those were not questions that troubled me at fourteen and fifteen. What concerned me was immersing myself in the lore and knowledge and arcana of my chosen sports and advancing into their highest, most aristocratic circles. The little kid with the worms and Wonder Bread and bamboo pole was ancient history. I had left him behind. Not too many more years would pass before it would dawn on me that perhaps it was he who had been out front all along.

II.

GROWING UP

CONFUSED

In the fall of 1957, when I was twenty-two, I guided deer hunters. My father had finally done what he had always wanted to do. He had quit commuting to his banking job in Manhattan and bought a sporting camp in Maine. He had been vacationing at Big Jim Pond Camps in western Maine for many years and had seen it sold in 1953 to Harry and Marge, a likable couple in their late thirties from Philadelphia, who, like my father, had visited Big Jim often as paying guests and–again like my father–saw it as the place where they wished they had always lived, the life they wished they had always lived.

But the life we wish for, once we get it, doesn't always turn out the way we had wished it would. It's one thing to arrive as a July guest at Big Jim's highway garage where the camp chore boy meets you, carts your luggage the quarter mile to the Dead River on a wheelbarrow, ferries you and your gear across the river in a big green scow, and drives you the mile and a half into camp in a 1931 Model A beach wagon. It's quite another to leave your home in Philadelphia late in April to go to Maine and get your camp ready to open at ice-out sometime in mid-May. At the garage on Maine Route 27, you find two or three feet of soggy snow still on the ground. You put on your snowshoes and lug your own gear to the ferry landing in backpacks. The scow is still in winter storage high up on the far bank to keep it safe from the spring runoff now spilling over the riverbanks and sending ice floes careening into the streamside trees. So you pull a canoe off the rack at the ferry landing and make your way across the muddy, roily water. No Model A awaits you on the far shore, so you put your snowshoes back on and slog into camp, whacking the wet, clingy snow off them with a stick every fourth or fifth step.

It's one thing to arrive and find a clean, airy log camp all ready for you, beds made, fresh towels on the bathroom racks, kerosene lamps filled and their wicks trimmed. It's another to open up and clean nine guest camps and a main lodge with dining room, kitchen, and lounge, scrub down the logs, mop the floors, do all that work sloshing back and forth in a camp yard awash in snowmelt and mud.

It's one thing to sit down to three meals a day served on red-and-white-checkered tablecloths. It's another to see that those three meals arrive on those tablecloths three times a day, meals cooked, more often than not, by hard-drinking woods cooks who maintain their delicate day-to-day balance only by nipping at the vanilla extract and who, once their thirst reaches desperation levels, disappear on weeklong benders, leaving Big Jim's proprietors to do the cooking themselves.

The hassles in the camp business are huge; the profits, minimal. Exactly what Harry and Marge's reasons for getting out were I don't know. But I do know that after their second season, they were ready to sell.

The only change when my parents took over was that the proprietors knew better what they were in for. The hassles remained huge; the profits, if any, remained minimal. The cooks still drank; so did the clientele, some more, some less. The fishermen usually turned up with just a modest quart or two of Canadian Club. The more boisterous hunting parties arrived with whole cases of beer and Four Roses mixed in with their gear. Many of them, it seemed to me, came to camp as much to drink as to hunt, maybe more to drink than to hunt. They were bumbling and helpless in the woods, careless with their rifles. They had not learned that you never pointed a rifle at anyone, no, not ever, not on purpose, not out of carelessness. Time after time, walking out on a trail to post a sport at a stand, I'd look back over my shoulder into the muzzle of a .30/06. It did not behoove me, the hired help, to tell my temporary bosses how to handle their firearms, so I would just quietly move out of the line of fire. When they heard a red squirrel scuttering through the leaves, they'd go into wild-eyed alert, rifles at the ready, safeties off. After those encounters with nondeer, I would remind my clients to check their safeties before we moved on.

The guides all carried rifles, ostensibly to hunt for themselves, but some of the deer that left camp tied onto car roofs and bearing out-of-state hunters' tags had been shot by guides. How many deer taken in the Maine woods each year were killed by guides rather than by their clients? Who can possibly say? The governing rule was: Don't ask, don't tell. But whatever the numbers, the result for a guide was, depending on the financial resources and generosity of the client, a more or less hefty tip. Money is always hard to come by in northern New England. That was one rationalization a guide could seize on for acquiescing in this sorry practice. Furthermore, he could tell himself, this hunting trip was costing his sport a small fortune. The man had paid for an out-of-state license; he'd spent several hundred dollars on gear and clothing; he was spending another few hundred to stay in camp for a week; and he was paying his guide's daily wages and keep. Wasn't he entitled to take home some meat and, if he (or rather his guide) was lucky, a nice head to hang on the wall?

I suppose this system could be regarded as just an extension of the local practice of having wives, sisters, grandmothers, and aunts buy hunting licenses so the men could use the extra tags and lay in a winter's supply of deer meat for an extended family. It provided a rare opportunity in the year when men accustomed to working too hard for too little could even the score a bit and earn some extra change fairly easily and pleasurably. They all loved to hunt, and they were good at it. But in my mind there was—and still is—a difference between shooting a second deer on Aunt May's tag to feed the family and shooting one for old Lou from downcountry, old Lou who might have waddled out of camp for two or three hours a day if he went out at all and then may well have spent most of his hunting time sitting in a pickup cab slamming back a few beers or nipping at his flask. One hunter hired Tom, a guide from the area, to go out with him to hunt for a week using a little outlying camp four miles away from our main camp. When they came back, the sport loaded a nice forkhorn buck on his car and went home. Tom told me the only time the guy staggered out of the camp the whole week was to go to the outhouse. Tom's reward, on top of his base pay, was a hundred-dollar tip, a respectable amount for those days; but if you consider he had to spend a week caretaking a puling drunk as well as shooting a deer for him, a hundred seems pretty paltry.

Contemptible as I may have found the whole enterprise, I was not above being drawn into it. On a day when I had no sports to guide, I went out hunting for camp meat. I would be staying on through the winter with Don, Big Jim's chief guide, caretaker, and genius of all work, and we wanted a deer or two hanging in the icehouse for the months ahead. What I wanted was a nice fat little doe or a spikehorn buck, but what I saw and got was an eight-point buck that weighed in at around 180 pounds. There was no snow on the ground yet, and I didn't even think about dragging him the mile down to the pond where I'd left my canoe. The next day, with the help of another guide and a one-wheel game carrier, I hauled the deer back to camp and strung him up on the rack.

It was Saturday, and because it was illegal to hunt on Sundays, most parties arrived and left camp on Sundays. That evening Joe Hunter, a short, beefy guy from someplace in Connecticut, caught me after supper to congratulate me on my hunting prowess.

"Helluva nice buck you got there, young fella," he said. "Congratulations!"

He took my hand and pressed it between both of his, giving me a broad wink at the same time. When he let go, I was holding a fifty and a twenty. "Yessiree," he said, "one helluva nice buck. Why, anybody'd be proud to take a trophy like that home now, wouldn't he?"

"Yes," I said, "I guess anybody would."

"Well, I thought we'd see eye to eye on that," he said. "Right?"

"Right," I agreed.

The next morning, when everybody was packed up and ready to leave, my mother came out of the kitchen to shake hands and bid the Connecticut crew farewell. When she saw my deer on Joe Hunter's car roof, she said, "Hey, that's Bob's deer."

And I said, "No, Mom, that's Mr. Hunter's deer."

"Oh, I see," my mother said, and she turned on her heel and went back to the kitchen.

Guiding deer hunters, I learned that *slob hunter* and *hunter* were sometimes synonymous. And from my little transaction with Joe Hunter, I learned that I was just one of the gang, one more slob among my fellow slobs. At age ten and from my vantage point atop Dick Hardy's chicken coop, I could hardly have imagined a more romantic and exalted role for myself than the one I actually stepped into twelve years later. There I was, a Maine guide, a latter-day deerslayer, a direct descendant of Natty Bumppo; but as my eight-point buck rolled out of the camp yard on the roof of Joe Hunter's car, romance, exaltation, and self-respect went with it, and shooting rats in Dick's hen yard began to look like a rather noble enterprise after all.

⚜

It seems I'd had the picture upside down and backward. It didn't take too long for me to realize that I preferred the company not of the sportsmen but of the local meat hunters who were out to stock up the family larder for the winter and made no bones about it. Those older men I first hunted with in Maine may have bent the letter of the law if they shot an extra deer on their wives' or sisters' licenses, but their delinquencies didn't make them criminal in my eyes then and still don't now. They knew and loved their native ground; they were modest, competent, fun to travel with. To hunt in their company was a joy; to hunt with most—certainly not all—of the sport hunters was an embarrassment and humiliation.

All of a sudden, the whole elaborate mythology of "sport" I had embraced in my boyhood and adolescence now seemed not only at odds with reality but more than a little silly. Did the gun editors at *Outdoor Life* and *Field & Stream* really need a trophy elk or a record-breaking bighorn sheep to keep body and soul together? A nontrophy elk would do just as well; so would lamb chops from the corner grocery. The more I saw of sport and sportsmen, the more I thought John Muir had things right: "I have precious little sympathy for the selfish propriety of civilized man," Muir wrote, "and if a war of races should occur between the wild beasts and Lord Man, I would be tempted to sympathize with the bears."

In these same years I came across José Ortega y Gasset's *Meditations on Hunting,* a text hunters sometimes cite to buttress their claims for the nobility, indeed, for the spiritual dimension, of their sport. In his chapter titled "The Ethics of Hunting," Ortega writes:

> *I have indicated that a sport is the effort which is carried out for the pleasure that it gives in itself and not for the transitory result that the effort brings forth. It follows that when an activity becomes a sport, whatever that activity may be, the hierarchy of its values becomes inverted. In utilitarian hunting the true purpose of the hunter, what he seeks and values, is the death of the animal. Everything else that he does before that is merely a means for achieving that end, which is its formal purpose. But in hunting as a sport this order of means to end is reversed. To the sportsman the death of the game is not what interests him; that is not his purpose. What interests him is everything that he had to do to achieve that death—that is, the hunt. . . . If one were to present the sportsman with the death of the animal as a gift he would refuse it. What he is after is having to win it, to conquer the surly brute through his own effort and skill with all the extras that this carries with it: the immersion in the countryside, the healthfulness of the exercise, the distraction from his job, and so on and so forth.*

*In all of this, the moral problem of hunting has
not been resolved, although it must be taken into account. We have not reached ethical perfection in
hunting, not in the least. One never achieves perfection
in anything, and perhaps it exists precisely so that
one can never achieve it, as happens with cardinal
points. Its purpose is to orient our conduct and to
allow us to measure the progress accomplished. . . .*

There were only two points I found I could give assent
to in this central passage: "the moral problem of hunting
has not been resolved," and "we have not reached ethical
perfection in hunting." But if ethical imperfection and ir-
resolution of the moral problem of hunting were to be my
fate, then both my own experience and just about everything Ortega had to say convinced me I would rather be
ethically imperfect and morally unresolved in the company of those utilitarian hunters Ortega treats with such
condescension. It is not, after all, the death of the animal
the utilitarian hunter seeks but the food the death of the
animal makes available. Utilitarian hunters always ac-
cept and give "the death of the animal" as a gift because
sharing the fruits of a successful hunt is part of the utilitarian hunter's responsibility to his or her family and
community. For the utilitarian hunter, the kill is a moment, both joyous and solemn, in which he gives thanks
for the gift of food he has received. It is the utilitarian
hunter dependent on the hunt for sustenance who will
have the greatest knowledge of, and respect for, his wild
brethren and whose culture will make that knowledge

and respect manifest in its arts, rituals, myths, and day-to-day behavior.

If hunting was an honorable pursuit at all, I began to feel, then its honor derived not from its sporting nature but from its roots in subsistence. If there was such a thing as a hunting aristocracy in the New World, it derived from the Native Americans. It went back to roots that reached farther and deeper into the human past than the peerage of any duke or baron or the feudal system that had spawned their ranks. It went back to survival, to the hunt for food. The Penobscot, the Blackfoot, and the Athabaskan all hunted to feed themselves and their families.

But in Ortega's Europe? The tie with subsistence was lost long ago, except among the poachers who continued to hunt for food in defiance of their supposed betters for whom the hunt was but one more form of amusement. Not only did Ortega scorn the utilitarian hunter, but he also looked back with nostalgia on a feudal order in which hunting was a privilege reserved for the aristocracy.

> *In periods . . . which were not revolutionary and in which, avoiding false utopias, people relied on things as they really were, not only was hunting a privilege respected by all, but those on the bottom demanded it of those on top, because they saw in hunting, especially in its superior forms—the chase, falconry, and the battue—a vigorous discipline and an opportunity to show courage, endurance, and skill, which are the attributes of the genuinely powerful person.*

How, I wondered then and continue to wonder, can the battue be perceived, by any stretch of the imagination, as "an opportunity to show courage, endurance, and skill"? The duke rounds up all the peasants at his disposal; the duke's huntsman lines all those peasants up at one end of the duke's woods; the duke stations himself and all the counts and lords in the neighborhood along the borders of the woods; the beaters go thrashing through the bush, flushing every deer, dove, and hare out into the open; and the dukes and the counts, sitting in their swivel chairs, blaze away at anything that runs, crawls, or flies. Granted, the beaters may need a little courage if their assignment is to plunge into dense underbrush and drive out a tiger that may decide his best option is to eat a beater or two rather than run past the muzzle of the raja's rifle. But what–apart from money and the power to order people around–is required of the hunter?

Or how about this: The duke buys a plane ticket to Anchorage and finds himself a bush pilot. The bush pilot takes the duke up in his plane and runs a wolf to the point of exhaustion. Then the duke shoots the wolf out the plane window. The bush pilot needs the skill to fly his plane, but what does the hunter need, apart from the money to pay the pilot's fee? (This dismal practice, once legal in Alaska, was outlawed there in 1972. However, initiatives to reinstate at least aerial spotting and pursuit of wolves continue to come up in the Alaskan legislature.)

Chasing wolves in an airplane was not, of course, what Ortega understood by "the chase." I assumed what he meant was riding to hounds, hordes of horsey barbarians yoicksing along behind a pack of dogs whose mission in life is to chase a fox to the point of exhaustion. Ridiculous and depraved as the whole business seemed to me, I had to admit, grudgingly, that bounding over the countryside on a horse behind a pack of yelping hounds took no little skill and, at times, may have called for endurance and daring, which, however, is a far cry from courage.

And what about falconry? However quaint, medieval, and—again—feudal falconry may seem to non-European ears, no one can deny endurance and skill to the bird; nor can I imagine how even the most pastoral of sensibilities could fail to thrill at the sight of what may be nature's most exalted hunters.

> *I caught this morning morning's minion, king-*
>   *dom of daylight's dauphin, dapple-dawn-drawn*
>   *Falcon, in his riding*
>   *Of the rolling level underneath him steady air,*
>   *and striding*
> *High there, how he rung upon the rein of a*
>   *wimpling wing*
> *In his ecstasy! Then off, off forth on swing,*
>   *As a skate's heel sweeps smooth on a bow-bend:*
>   *the hurl and gliding*
>   *Rebuffed the big wind. My heart in hiding*
> *Stirred for a bird,—the achieve of, the mastery of*
>   *the thing!*

Who can blame poor earthbound man, the plodding hunter who has to put one weary foot in front of another, for want-

ing to ally himself with that bird, to soar and to be oneself–
in one's own body–the arrow, the spear, the missile that
strikes its prey dead like a bolt out of the blue? This syn-
ergy of human and bird taps into some deep longing we
have to be as pure, guileless, and guiltless in the hunt as
the falcon is, a longing that is not touched–or at least not
touched to anywhere near the same degree–by hunting
with dogs. Dogs are so much creatures of our making that
we do not enter the wild as completely through them as we
do through the bird. Rich, satisfying, and loving as the tie
between human and dog in the field is, that human–canine
team is a team of domestic animals working together to
draw the wild animal into its range. The dog literally
brings the game to hand, and if it is possible to picture a
line that separates the wild from the domestic, the dog and
hunter working together bring the wild over to their side.
Perhaps no animal can take us across the line and totally
into the wild, but the falcon comes closer to doing that than
any other creature humans hunt with. The falcon still
hunts for itself, not for its master. The dog is of our world;
the falcon is of its own. To hunt with the bird, we have to
leave our domestic arrangements behind and enter realms
in which, in reality, we cannot even move or survive. We
cannot fly, and we are without talons. We are wingless and
weaponless. We have mediocre eyesight, dull hearing, virtually no sense of smell at all. We are slow, clumsy, noisy
creatures. Without our brains, without the gadgetry they
devise and the knowledge they are able to acquire and
store up about our prey, we would not be able to hunt at all.
So to hunt with the falcon is indeed to engage in a superior

form of hunting, but at the same time it is not to hunt at all. It is to let the bird hunt and to hunt with it vicariously, only as spectators and only in our imaginations. Curiously, in this superior form of hunting, we are at our farthest remove from the hunt. We do not strike the game ourselves. We participate in the hunt metaphorically. The bird is a figure of speech in the flesh, and at the same moment that it is almost an abstraction, merely a speck in the sky, it carries us farther into the life of the wild than we can reach ourselves, farther into a state in which consciousness and action are one and we feel a part of—not alien to—the vast, complex intelligence of the natural order. Falconry would seem to be as much about the poetic capacities of the human mind as it is about the hunt.

But for me to carry on like this about the glories of falconry is, I suppose, patently silly. I've never hunted with birds. All I know of falconry I know secondhand from writers, such as Dan O'Brien and Steve Bodio. All I know firsthand of raptors is what I know from watching the hawks, kestrels, ospreys, bald eagles, and northern harriers that inhabit my part of the world. But if the hints I get from those sources are accurate, then Ortega may be as right about falconry as he is wrong about the battue.

That's what reading Ortega is like. My reactions to him today remain as mixed as they were when I first read him some forty years ago: irritation at his neofeudal posing and his pomposities, gratitude for the questions he either asks directly himself or indirectly obliges his reader to confront. What is the place of the kill in hunting? Is killing in the hunt different from killing a domestic animal in the slaughterhouse or the barnyard? If so, how is it different? Granted that we have not and cannot achieve ethical perfection in hunting (or in anything else), can the unattainable goal of perfection serve, as Ortega suggests, as a cardinal point for orienting our conduct? And assuming we do in fact so orient our conduct, where between the extremes of unattainable perfection and wanton, mindless killing do we draw the line of acceptable conduct?

Ortega addresses this question and comes up with what he thinks a perfectly satisfactory answer: "The exemplary moral spirit of the sporting hunter, that manner of feeling, of taking up and practicing hunting, is a very precise line, below which fall innumerable forms of hunting that are deficient modes of this occupation; deficient in the aspects of dexterity, boldness, and effort, or simply in the moral aspect." Agreed. However, the line below which we find deficient modes seems not precise to me at all but rather a large, gray zone. For Ortega, the chase and the battue fall well above that line; for me, below. Indeed, the only mode of hunting he describes that seems to me adequate in its requirements of dexterity, effort, and moral aspect is "that in which the hunter, alone in the mountains, is at the same time the person who discovers the prey, the one who pursues it, and the one who fells it." *Boldness*, like *courage*, seems another of Ortega's misapplied terms. How many sport hunters in the industrialized world go out armed only with a lance to hunt polar bears?

My differences with Ortega here are not attributable entirely to our different cultures. My culture is awash in practices that are at odds with that lone-hunter ideal and that enjoy not only the approval of many hunters but also the sanction of the law. Here in my state of Maine, for instance, bear-hunting guides put bucketfuls of stale jelly doughnuts out in the woods to draw the bears. Then they station a sport in a tree stand, and the sport pots the bear when it comes to the bait. So much for courage, endurance, and skill. The other legally sanctioned method for hunting bears is running them with dogs. The argument goes that black bears in Maine are extremely wary creatures and that without the aid of bait or dogs most bear hunters would go home empty-handed.

Well, so be it. Just how much help in the form of improved technology (guns, binoculars, scope sights, airplanes, helicopters, snowmobiles) and of guides, beaters, bait, and/or dogs are we willing to concede a hunter and still consider him a hunter? At what point does he become just a contemptible ignoramus who buys the use of other people's skills and machinery to put him in a position not even to hunt but simply to kill something? The absolute nadir in this department is the canned hunt in which a "hunter" guns down a big-game animal in fenced-in fields that make escape for the animal impossible. Depravity at that extreme rouses just about anyone's disgust, but in the large gray zone where things are not so clear it probably behooves none of us to be too self-righteous. A man who makes his own bow and arrows and hunts with them may well feel the same disapprobation for me and my ancient Remington .22 as I feel for the bear baiters.

These wildly differing judgments on what constitutes ethical hunting behavior all stem from the undeniable fact that most of us who hunt do not *need* to hunt. We cannot say with the Abenaki hunter, "I have killed you because I need your skin for my coat and your flesh for my food. I have nothing else to live on." This lack of need wakens in us what Ortega calls "the hint of criminal suspicion which claws the hunter's conscience." "*Every good hunter,*" he writes, "*is uneasy in the depths of his conscience when faced with the death he is about to inflict on the enchanting animal.* He does not have the final and firm conviction that his conduct is correct. But neither, it should be understood, is he certain of the opposite."

I assume that *good* here means "ethical" and that *hunter* means "sport hunter." So the sentence says: Every ethical sport hunter is uneasy, and he is uneasy because he cannot speak with the Abenaki hunter. He has just about everything else under the sun to live on, from artichokes and avocados to zabiglione; just about everything from Gore-Tex to silk long johns to wear. No wonder his conscience troubles him. He's got a refrigerator, a freezer, and a pantry stuffed full of food at home. So what rationale can he come up with to justify this death he is about to inflict?

Ortega's answer: "*. . . the principle which inspires hunting for sport is that of artificially perpetuating, as a possibility for man, a situation which is archaic in the highest degree: that early state in which, already human, he still lived within the orbit of animal existence.*"

But why bother? What are the benefits of artificially perpetuating that archaic situation? From what I saw of sport hunting at Big Jim, the benefits seemed few and far between, if there were any at all. Even the side benefits of

sport hunting, the "extras" Ortega mentions, were conspic-
uously absent. It was the rare sport hunter who spent enough
time in the countryside or was attentive enough to it to be
immersed in it; it was the rare sport hunter who walked
enough in a day to get any healthful exercise. As for Ortega's
main point and presumably sport hunting's major benefit–
artificially perpetuating that early state in which we humans,
self-aware, lived within the orbit of animal existence–what
is that for any sport hunter living in the industrialized
world and fed by industrialized agriculture but a self-de-
luding, atavistic pipe dream? When we go into the field
pretending we can live in the orbit of animal existence with
the same authenticity as the ancient subsistence hunter,
we know we are kidding ourselves. We know we are at some
level killing for "fun," no matter what ingenious gloss we
may choose to put on our killing. And so that hint of criminal suspicion continues to claw at the hunter's conscience.

❦

Deer were plentiful in Maine in the late 1950s and into
the 1960s; the hunting was good. My father could book his
camps solid right through deer season. Those six weeks
each fall paid the bills. They made up for the so-so fishing
in spring and the dog days of summer. But crucial as they
were to Big Jim's economic survival, my father never
looked forward to them and was always happy to see the
last hunter go down the road. He never said as much, but I
suspect that he had neither encouraged nor discouraged
me from hunting because of his own ambivalence about it.

My own limited experience with sport hunting had left me, too, less than enthusiastic, but in January 1958, I was drafted into the army and soon found myself stationed in Berlin, Germany, where I had little occasion even to think about hunting for food or for sport or to sort out my thinking about either activity. Several years of graduate study and teaching in both Europe and at home followed, and when I returned to rural life in 1971, married now and, the following year, the father of an infant son, my wife and I turned not to hunting, fishing, and foraging but to gardening and small-scale animal husbandry to supply many of our food needs.

III.

VENTURES IN THE
STOCK MARKET

F or well over a decade, almost all the meat my family
and I ate came neither from the supermarket nor from
hunting. I hunted not at all in those years and fished
nowhere near enough, but then what could ever be
enough? We had an occasional mess of trout. Trolling a
streamer just after the last, tinkling candle ice disappeared
from Varnum Pond in May sometimes yielded a landlocked
salmon or togue big enough to make a generous feed for
Rita, our son, Greg, me, and company. Once Greg was old
enough to join me, he and I spent many June evenings
casting plugs along the shorelines of warm-water ponds,
and if we failed to snag a two- or three-pound largemouth,
we could always drift back out into the middle of the pond
and catch a dozen or more white perch on spinners and
worms. In July and August I would spend a few evenings
fishing shallow, weedy ponds for pickerel.

But foraging of any kind took a backseat to agriculture.

Rita, too, had been studying and teaching for several years when we met in Boston in 1969. After one more year of academe, we moved to a falling-down farm in western Maine. We suddenly owned 110 acres, most of them woods but about 15 acres in fields. Translating books from the German yielded an extremely modest cash income, and we turned to our land to provide us with all of our fuel and much of our food.

Rita took charge of the kitchen garden, which is still giving us the glory of fresh peas, lettuce, basil, parsley, zucchini, summer squash, strawberries, raspberries, broccoli, green peppers, and tomatoes as they mature, then potatoes, cabbages, carrots, beets, and frozen vegetables all winter long. I took on animal husbandry. We started with chickens, then moved on to sheep, ducks, and, once, a beef animal.

Raising and slaughtering your own meat animals may at least suggest to you the possibility of becoming either a hunter or a vegetarian. I was about to revise that last sentence and say it's just the slaughtering that will, but that isn't quite right either, though it's surely the moment of slaughter that's most likely to raise doubts about the whole meat-raising, meat-eating enterprise. Slaughter–to articulate the utterly obvious–is what transforms a live creature into a dead one. My point in belaboring the self-evident here is not that slaughtering an animal kills it but rather that slaughter does not instantly transform the live animal into meat. Once the animal has become *meat* it is no longer an animal. Meat is like lumber. We can saw it and cut it and carve it into shapes that suit our needs and convenience: two-by-fours, two-by-eights, planks, boards, chops, roasts, steaks, stew meat. Meat is not a fellow creature whom we, with our own hands, push across the line from life to death. The moment of slaughter, no matter how quick, humane, and painless you make it, is a moment when you see life go out in an animal's eye.

Rita soon learned that witnessing that transition was not for her. The first fall we had chickens, she helped me hold the first one on the chopping block while I lopped its head off with the ax. The bird's death was instantaneous, but the headless body running and flapping wildly around the yard and the guillotined head lying on the grass was a gory little drama she did not care to attend again. Once the transition to meat had been made, indeed, even the transition to an immobile carcass, she could stomach the plucking and drawing. She could stuff the dead, decapitated birds into hot water to loosen up the feathers for plucking; she could tolerate the stench of sodden chicken, an aroma in which the smell of even a clean, well-tended henhouse— that mix of chicken manure, wood shavings, sawdust, and poultry dander—rises to the nose intensified by heat and dampness. Rita could put up with that. She could reach up inside the still-warm bodies and haul out fistfuls of lung, liver, and heart, the orderly tangle of intestines, the cloaca often loaded with its charge of eggs, the shell almost hard on the first one, the second complete and whole but encased only in a transparent membrane, and so on back up the line, each egg smaller and smaller until the far end of the chain disappeared in mystery.

She could do everything but the killing, which she left to me. I read USDA and University of Maine Extension Service pamphlets on the housing, feeding, doctoring, slaughtering, dressing, canning, freezing, and cooking of poultry. I read that the quickest, most humane way to kill chickens was to hang them by their feet and run an ice pick from just under the lower mandible up into the brain. Ridiculous. You have to catch them, string them up, grab them by the head, then probe for the brain like a flustered medical technician trying to hit an elusive vein in a patient's forearm. Chicken brains are small and hard to find, but they are large enough to tell chickens that a man grabbing them by the feet and hanging them upside down from a chest-high limb on a red maple tree is up to no good. I soon abandoned the ice pick for a sharp knife, with which I could slice off heads much more quickly than I could locate a brain. But that still did not do away with the catching and stringing up, all of which did nothing but intensify and lengthen both the chickens' and my distress.

The advantages this USDA approach had over the ax and chopping block seemed to me utterly nonexistent, and I concluded that the advice in the pamphlet must have been written by an engineer in a big meatpacking plant where upside-down chickens trundled by a guy with an ice pick and, once they had been debrained, were then plopped into the defeathering vat, which has been described to me as something like a huge front-loading washing machine in which a combination of warm water and intricately interacting rubber flails whack and tumble the feathers off the birds.

Eventually I learned that the quickest, most efficient way to kill a chicken is to grab it by the head and crank, as though you were starting up a Model T. The bird's body, spinning in a circle, snaps its neck instantly. Do this too vigorously, and the body will go flying, leaving you standing there with the head in your hand.

Unfortunately, sheep cannot be picked up by the head and spun around in the air. I remember reading about one shepherd who went out onto the sheep pasture with his .22 rifle, shot in the head the lambs he wanted to butcher, then proceeded to dress them out. This method was surely easy on the sheep. There they were, merrily grazing away, and the next second they were dead. What I didn't like about it was the idea of half a dozen dead animals lying around in the field while I skinned and paunched out one, then another, then another. So I would wrestle lambs out of the pen one at a time, tie them to a tree, shoot them in the head, slit their throats, then dress them out, also one at a time. If something unforeseen came up or if I just grew weary of blood and sheepskins and heaps of guts, I could quit. There were no dead sheep lying out in the field that had to be dealt with right away.

But this procedure was far from elegant and far from easy on the sheep. The first lamb to the slaughter resisted being dragged out just on principle. The ones that followed could smell the blood and didn't like it. They squirmed, balked, dug in their heels, fought for their lives. The morality of slaughtering demands that we not force animals into a state of mortal terror. Industrialized meat processing does. In fact, just about everything involved in industrial meat production reduces animals to products and deprives them of their animality. Production-line slaughtering is

merely the culminating step in a process that has denied
these animals anything resembling an animal life.

But I couldn't be too proud of how I ushered my lambs
and sheep out of this life either. Hit in the head with a .22
bullet, they plopped instantly to the ground, and, presumably, their consciousness and their ordeal was over. But
getting to that point was an ordeal, both for them and for
me, and if I botched the killing, the ordeal for us both was
worse. One fall I attempted stunning the lambs with the
poll of a single-bitted ax. With the first three, I aimed well,
smacking the animals cleanly and squarely on the head,
and they dropped as neatly as if shot. But the fourth
squirmed just enough to avoid the direct blow; the ax
glanced off the side of its head; and I was confronted with
a frantic, suffering, wounded creature I had to dispatch as
best I could. My best was pitifully inadequate. The sheep's
writhings made an accurate second blow difficult. The ax
crushed its nose, then its left front leg. It was down on its
side now, flailing with its legs, strangling on the rope that
held it to the tree, its body arching and snapping. The
fourth blow finally accomplished what the first should
have, and the body lay twitching at my feet. My hands
trembling, I cut the rope and slit the animal's throat, and as
its still-beating heart pumped its blood out onto the
ground, I took a few minutes to anoint my stupid head with
self-loathing before I wiped the ax clean and went back up
to the house to get the .22. I've never used an ax since for
anything but cutting and splitting wood.

The first year we had the sheep, I'd taken the few lambs
we had to a local butcher, a farmer who had converted a

corner of his barn into a small-scale meatpacking plant sparkling with all the stainless steel the state inspectors require of anyone who cuts meat for the public. Hiring out the slaughtering and butchering of your animals is not quite as comfortable as buying meat in the supermarket, but it's a good second best. You truck your animals to the butcher's holding pen, and a few days later you pick up neatly wrapped packages labeled "loin chops, leg of lamb, stew meat." The hides, the heads, the hooves, the rumen, the reticulum, the omasum and abomasum—none of that you have to deal with. You get an almost free ride. You deliver an animal; you pick up meat. You don't have to pay the price of killing an animal that does not want to die.

On the November afternoon when I delivered my lambs, the farmer and his two burly teenage sons were working full tilt. The boys wrestled two pigs into the slaughter room, slung chains around their hind legs, yanked them squealing up into the air with pulleys, and slit their throats. The boys were quick and efficient; the animals' pain was brief; but, I felt, even that brief pain was too much, and the thought of my lambs flying upside down to their deaths troubled me enough that I resolved that evening to do my own slaughtering from then on.

Surely my one ax-killed lamb fared much worse with me than it would have with the farmer and his boys, and even the lambs and sheep I killed cleanly with a .22 bullet in the head still had to be hauled out to the killing tree. My sheep were spared the truck ride and the night in the holding pen, but whether they died easier, gentler deaths at my hands than they would have at the farmer's slaughterhouse is a toss-up. All I could say with certainty was that I assumed personal responsibility for those deaths. If we were going to eat meat, then we would be the ones who killed the animals that became our meat.

Beyond that, we also knew that our animals had lived animal lives. Until that instant when I broke their necks, our chickens had it good. They lived lives so blissful that, watching them, I could almost wish I were a chicken myself. When I opened the henhouse door in the morning, they came down the little ramp slowly, turning their heads from side to side, as dignified as Queen Elizabeth deplaning in Bombay on a goodwill tour. Unlike Dick Hardy's chickens in their rat-infested coop, our birds could wander at will. There were no fences in their lives. We had 110 acres, more or less, not just 1½ or 2. Our neighbors were far enough away that our chickens would never get into their gardens or crap on their lawns. The birds fanned out and started grazing like cows, nibbling at grass and snatching up grasshoppers. When I tore down our sagging back porch to replace it, the chickens soon made themselves dust baths in the dry, weedless soil, and in the heat of summer days, just around lunchtime, several of them would gather there and chat as they wriggled down into their tubs. Chickens may not be terribly clever, but their conversation wears much better than that of some people. Their prattling and clucking is companionable rather than intrusive, and when they have something urgent or important to communicate, they don't beat around the bush. Their shrieks of fear are unmistakable. The pride they take in their own workmanship when they've produced an egg lifts the spirit (Put-put-put-BAWP! I've laid an EGG!). I loved our roosters' bravado and braggadocio as they strutted around like Wyatt Earp in Kansas City, their fierce possessiveness and territoriality as they flew at me, tore at my shins with their spurs, then swaggered off, hitching up their gun belts and muttering to themselves, "I guess I showed that sonofabitch. I guess I kicked his ass."

But enviable as the lives of our chickens may have been in a chickenly context (just think what any poor debeaked battery hen would have given to trade places with one of ours), even the best of chicken lives is still severely limited. Chicken society is, for instance, patriarchal to the core. All the males seem interested in is fucking, fighting, and keeping the hens in a state of cringing submission. The cocks' sex drive is prodigious, but they're always in such a terrible hurry they make lousy lovers. You really can't blame the hens for squawking blue murder and trying to get away. And then even though the hens are quite civil to each other most of the time, I never noticed anything I'd call feminine solidarity among them, and sociopathic ills do turn up now and then. The freedom, fresh air, and wholesome food our birds enjoyed seemed to keep nastiness to a minimum, though occasionally some poor creature would be cannibalized and wind up defeathered, bloody, and dead.

The sheep did not beat up on each other, though occasionally our alpha ram would take it into his hard and bony head to clobber me from behind. Sheep are supposed to be stupid, but never once did our ram attack me head-on. He bided his time until my back was turned and I was bending over, maybe patching a hole in the fence or picking up a water bucket but in any case presenting an ideal and off-balance target. Such behavior would seem, on the face of it, a manifestation of crass ingratitude and not at all in a sheep's best interests. After all, who was it who came down to the sheep shed two and three and sometimes more times a day in the dead of winter bringing fresh water, busting open another bale of hay, and doling out a ration of grain for everybody in the joint? Why would that ram want to make an enemy of me unless he already knew that I was like the witch in "Hansel and Gretel," just fattening up his lambs for the kill? Whatever his "reasons," at least some of them were correct. I was in fact the wolf in shepherd's clothing. If he had succeeded in butting me out of his world altogether, I could not have killed and eaten his progeny. On the other hand, without me or the likes of me, he and his progeny would have starved to death.

Cattle and *chattel* not only rhyme; they also come from the same root. The path back through Middle English *catel* to Middle French and medieval Latin *capitale* is straight and clear. Our little flock of sheep represented our capital; they were, in a sense, money in the bank; and though we owned no shares in the J. P. Morgan bank, we owned stock and were, in a different but still related sense, stockholders. Our sheep's lives were not their own but ours, our property. We determined if and when they would be born and when they would die. The purpose of their lives was to carry our purpose for them. "Cattle raising," Ortega writes, "is a relationship between man and animal that was invented by man and begins in him; if we were to represent it graphically we would have to draw an arrow that goes from man to the animal. . . . But hunting . . . is a relationship that certain animals impose on man, to the point where not trying to hunt them demands the intervention of our deliberate will. The graphic symbol for the hunting relationship would have to be the inverse of that which represents cattle raising; the arrow would have to be drawn emerging from the animal." And a few paragraphs farther on: "Man cannot re-enter Nature except by temporarily rehabilitating that part of himself which is still an animal. And this, in turn, can be achieved only by placing himself in relation to another animal. But there is no animal, pure animal, other than the wild one, and the relationship with him is the hunt."

Cattle are a human invention, a product of genetic engineering. They are as much a part of our technology as the moldboard plow and frozen food. We invented them so that we'd be sure to have a coat to wear and flesh to eat in case we proved either inept or unlucky hunters. A sheep is surely a more reliable source of meat and a warm jacket than some deer running around loose out there in the woods, God knows where. But then on the heels of the invention of the sheep come other inventions that help sustain the sheep: the cleared fields, the mowing machines, the balers. So in providing us with a certain food supply, our cattle make our lives safer but not simpler; and the "pure" animals, the wild ones that carry only their own purposes, not ours, become potential rivals to our invented animals.

❧

I have to admit that in my stockholding years I gave next to no thought to these convoluted and subtle issues and certainly lost no sleep over them. Whatever thought Rita and I did give to them was largely upbeat and cheerful. What we could see and rejoice in was that our little flock of sheep enjoyed a quality of life not often granted to livestock in the world of agribusiness. They had the free run of several bottomland acres that kept them handsomely fed from mid-May until the first snows and that they, in return, kept neatly trimmed and free of brush; they could come and go from their shed at will; they had fresh air, sunshine, a trout stream running through their pasture. In winter they were fed and watered, and because they were few, they were not crowded in their winter quarters. What more could a sheep want? Until the day of reckoning came, they had it as good as any domestic animal destined to be human food could have it. We prided ourselves in thinking that our sheep, chickens, and ducks could live out their animal natures in almost as much freedom as wild animals could live out theirs. Rita may not have been able to crank chickens' heads off or slaughter sheep, but she could assent to the philosophical and ecological soundness of our small-scale, family-sized, subsistence-style agriculture. Greg understood from earliest childhood that our livestock were not pets and playmates, like our dogs and cats, but animals that we would kill to eat. In fall we gathered in the garden crops; we slaughtered the year's lambs.

For reasons I still do not understand yet remain grateful for, our sheep were never attacked by the coyotes and

bears that sometimes descended on the flock of our neighbor just half a mile away. I was grateful for the unaccount-
able choosiness of those predators, because it let me
sidestep a moral decision I much preferred not having to
make. Would I, like my neighbor, after losing a sheep to a
bear, have called in the game warden and the local bear
hunter with his dogs? Probably. In theory, I was willing to
put up with what I considered some inevitable and justified attrition. We sheep and human beings had invaded the
bears' territory, so it seemed only fair that we provide them
with an occasional meal. Then, too, the bears, being wild,
were "pure," obviously of a much higher order than our
cloddish, degenerate sheep. As I mentioned, however, I
could afford this high-minded view because it was my
neighbor's sheep, not mine, that were falling prey to these
neighborhood carnivores.

How limited my high-mindedness was I found out
whenever pure, wild animals did trespass on my property.
In not infrequent moments of absentmindedness, I would
forget, come sunset, to close the small door the chickens
used to go into and out of the henhouse. Most of the time
my negligence would go unpunished, and when I went
down to let the ladies out the next morning, I would find
them already clucking around outside, their numbers
undiminished. But occasionally, on mornings when I was-
n't so lucky, I'd go down to the henhouse and find only two-
thirds the original number of chickens out enjoying an
early breakfast. Inside, I would find mayhem. The upset-
ting thing about a raccoon raid on a chicken coop is that a
raccoon does not behave the way any sensible, rational

creature should. He does not just come in, take what he needs, and leave. I could live with that. I could happily set aside a chicken every month or so and say, "All right. I eat chicken. You eat chicken. Here's a chicken for you. See you next month."

But raccoons don't work that way. People who think raccoons are cute with their clever little hands and their Lone-Ranger masks and washing their food the way any civilized person should—well, those people are dead wrong. They have never gazed into the black pit that is a raccoon's soul. Raccoons are savage and bloodthirsty. They have no scruples. If they find an open henhouse, they leave any last scrap of decency and humanity they may have ever possessed at the door. They tear into those hapless hens in a frenzy of bloodletting. They don't even eat what they kill. They take a head off here, bite into a jugular vein there, leave torn and tattered carcasses tossed right and left.

Sometimes they pull off their murderous work in utter silence. They work with the highly trained, deadly stealth of a Navy SEAL, picking off one hen, then another so swiftly and silently that the victim's neighbor doesn't even know that Cousin Harriet has just been yanked off the roost to her doom. Other times they wade in like an ax murderer, swinging right and left and rousing every bird in the place into a squawking, wing-flapping hubbub.

Then I wake up, yanked bolt upright in bed like a puppet on a string.

"Jesus," I say, "coon!"

I dive out of bed, grab a flashlight and the old Remington .22 from its corner in the ell, and race down to the chicken coop barefoot in the frost. Raccoons are especially fond of killing chickens on early fall nights with heavy frost. The coon has heard me coming and managed to get out of the henhouse before I arrive, but he hasn't moved quickly enough to get away. He may be under the coop, scrunched way back out of reach where the rear sill log comes down to within a few inches of the ground, or he may be up in the little red maple or the ancient apple tree just a few yards from the coop. Wherever he is, I pick up those amazingly yellow reflector eyes of his with the flashlight and shoot him.

Why? Surely not to "protect" my chickens from future raids. The easiest, most reliable way to do that was to remember to shut the door to the coop. Simple.

No, if I chose to think about it (which I didn't), I just had it in for raccoons. Not only did they kill chickens if given a chance, they also destroyed our corn patch, and they destroyed it with the same random savagery they brought to chicken killing. They worked their way up and down the rows of corn, tearing down ear after ear, taking one or two bites out of them, mauling them, then tossing them aside.

Now, if there is any vegetable that I regard as a near deity, it is sweet corn. Garden-fresh sweet corn is right up there with garden-fresh asparagus. Anyone or anything that destroys and defiles our corn patch is The Enemy. And remember, the season for corn is brief. In Maine corn needs all the summer we have to mature. Like proud parents, we cluck fondly over the infant stalks poking their green leaves up toward the June sky. We are gratified when our corn grows on schedule and is, as local folk wisdom says it ought to be, knee-high by the Fourth of July. If a fluke windstorm flattens our corn, I right each stalk, firm the dirt around its roots, and with stakes and string weave a web of support that will help the weakened stalks regain their hold on earth and withstand any further assaults from the wind.

Along about mid-August, when the ears are filling out and firming up, I go down to the garden and cheer them on. "Looking good," I say. "Hang in there. You're coming along famously." Inevitably I'll jump the gun and pick a few ears before they're really ready. The kernels will be disappointingly small, pale, and watery, and Rita will say, "You just can't learn to wait, can you?"

And I'll say, "No, no, I can't!"

But then, a week or ten days later, when the corn really is ripe, utter bliss descends. Every evening just before suppertime I go down to the garden and pick half a dozen ears. I shuck them on the back porch, put them in the steamer basket, take them inside, and put them on the stove. The total time expired from the moment of picking to the moment of eating is rarely more than fifteen or twenty minutes. Language is a poor, sad, cerebral instrument: It cannot begin to convey the taste of those plump kernels exploding sweetly in the mouth. Butter and salt are superfluous. Would you put ketchup on caviar? We roll this ambrosial mash around in our mouths the way wine tasters savor a prize vintage. We let it reach every conceivable taste bud; we inhale deeply; we look heavenward in gratitude. We sigh. Any raccoon that would deprive me of this annual apogee of joy is in trouble. As I said, the season for corn is brief. You get one chance at it, and if the coons beat you to it, you don't get any. It's not like lettuce. You can't re-plant it and get some more in a few weeks.

But even worse than corn depredation, if anything could conceivably be worse, was the death of the ducks. Someone gave us a few Muscovy ducks. Muscovies are ex-otics and are exotic looking; different individuals differ radically in their plumage. But they all seem to share a quiet, amiable nature that makes them pleasant to have waddling around the place. And when Thanksgiving or Christmas or any high holiday comes around, *caneton à l'orange* makes a main course that may not surpass sweet corn fresh from the garden but surely runs it a very close second, so close in fact that ducks might even be consid-ered sweet corn on the hoof.

So raccoon inroads on our ducks seemed to me even more criminal than corn and henhouse raids not only be-cause I prized the ducks so highly myself but also because we had only a few of them—nowhere near as many as we had hens or ears of corn—and because they were an utterly helpless prey and much more difficult to protect. Unlike the corn patch, they were not stationary, and I could not, as I fairly quickly learned to do for the corn, run a few strands of lightly electrified wire around them. And unlike the chickens, they did not return to roosts in a henhouse, where, if their owner only had wits enough to close the door, they were perfectly safe. At nightfall the ducks might settle down anywhere. In the morning I might find a heap of shredded duck, another victim of those black-masked commandos.

The only way I could have protected the ducks would have been to keep them in a fenced-in run and to shoo them into a predatorproof shelter at night. But that went against the grain. The ducks liked to wander, going down to the stream to jump in and paddle around, then coming back up to socialize a bit with the chickens and eat a bit of cracked corn. Committing the ducks to a penned-in life up on the high ground away from the water seemed all wrong. I wanted them to roam at will, but if they roamed at will, they would be dead. We would be deprived both of their company and of our occasional *caneton à l'orange.*

An all-out war on raccoons was doomed to failure. The enemy had plenty of troops in reserve, and if that is indeed what this contest over the ducks would have to come to, I had to admit I had no stomach for it. I hope I have not created the impression here that I was out popping off raccoons right and left. During the fifteen or more years we kept chickens, I shot no more than three or four raccoons; and each time I did, I had yielded to what I can only call an unthinking, vengeful impulse, accomplishing nothing that would effectively protect the chickens yet destroying an animal that was just going about survival according to his own lights. If I could kill a raccoon that had killed my hens, would I—to pick up the question again—hesitate to kill a bear that was killing my sheep? Sheep are bigger than chickens. The loss of a sheep counts for more than the loss of a chicken or even of three or four chickens. I decided I probably would have hesitated for a couple of reasons. First, a bear is, in every sense, bigger than a raccoon. Not only is it physically bigger, a major project to deal with, a lot more meat, a big hide; but it is also symbolically bigger. Even for people as far removed from the wild as we modern, information-age humans are, it carries some totemic force; we feel ourselves members of a bear clan, scattered and broken though that clan may be, and we are reluctant to take the life of that ancestral animal merely because it has made a dent in our property. Then, too, the idea of calling in the bear hounds did not sit well with me. But my guess is that after two or three or four dead sheep, I would have put hesitation behind me and said, "Enough."

As I've said, I thought very little about these questions at the time, and my not declaring war on the raccoons was as much a practical decision as anything else. It was just a lot easier to stop keeping ducks, to be careful about the henhouse door, and to put up my two or three strands of wire than it was to run around barefoot in the frost at 3 A.M. armed with a flashlight and a .22. But in retrospect I realize that those occasional raccoon raids on my food sources, whether animal or vegetable, were teaching me—had I been open to the lesson—how ready I was both to demonize creatures that crossed me and to declare them vermin. "Ax murderers," I called those raccoons, "savage and bloodthirsty." On my own miniature scale, I had duplicated the responses of the stockmen who decided that wolves and coyotes should be shot, trapped, and poisoned out of existence because they sometimes killed sheep or cattle. One official definition of *vermin* is "an animal that competes with humans or domestic animals for food." This definition bloomed into a full, round, authoritative syllogism for me: All animals that compete with humans for food are vermin.

Raccoons compete with me for food. Therefore, raccoons are vermin.

I was so much in thrall to the force of this logic that I couldn't even imagine there were any scruples I should be scrupling about, nor did it occur to me, so oblivious was I, that I was in violation of the law. In Maine the raccoon is not vermin but a game animal. Raccoons are not outside the law but protected by it. In Maine, to shoot raccoons legally, you must (a) be in possession of a valid hunting license and (b) shoot them only between October 1 and December 31. But along with my regrets at having mindlessly violated the law come other regrets of a different order, chief among them being that I treated those coons as if they were indeed "vermin," in the same class as the Norway rats in Dick Hardy's chicken coop. I did not skin and eat those few raccoons. I did not tan their pelts. I picked them up by the tail and tossed them into the woods for the scavengers to eat, treating them with no more respect than I had the rats at Dick's place. So much a captive to my agriculturalist's purposes was I that I could not grant this creature the dignity that any real hunter would: to sustain his own life with the flesh of the creature whose life he had taken.

These experiences as a keeper and killer of domestic animals and as a sometime killer of wild animals that sometimes interfered with my keeping and killing of domestic ones might have moved me to take up a clear and principled position. I might have concluded that my role as a husbandman and the investment I had in my sheep and chickens had addled my brains and made me see the pure, wild raccoon as evil. If keeping and killing domestic ani-

mals could so distort my perceptions, then animal husbandry
must in itself be evil. Therefore, in a moment of blinding
clarity, I would see that only by renouncing meat altogether and clinging to the straight and narrow path of carrots
and oatmeal would I achieve consistency and salvation.

Well, I'm a slow study. No such revelations came my
way; and when Rita and I finally did kill off the last of our
sheep and chickens and give up keeping meat animals, we
were not prompted to do so by these moral dilemmas; nor
had we decided, on philosophical or any other grounds,
that we would be pure, principled vegetarians. Our motives
were largely practical: Writing and translating work was
demanding more and more of our time, and cutting back
on our consumption of red meat and eggs surely would do
our aging arteries no harm. We would not refuse meat offered to us, and if we had a hankering for meat, red or
white, we would not even feel we were stooping if we
bought a Thanksgiving turkey, a freezer lamb, or a quarter
of beef, especially if we bought it from a local grower
whose animals were raised as we had raised our own:
range-fed and running free.

If my years as a keeper of meat animals had given me
clarity on anything, it was only on my own confusion, on
my own muddled nature as herbivore and carnivore, as
sheep and tiger. I lived, and still live, both literally and
morally, in a fluid, ill-defined border territory between the
wild and the domestic, between the tilled soil and the
beasts of the field. Rural Maine is like that. Garden, pasture, and forest, lettuce, sheep, and coyotes, the works of
humans and the works of nature interlock like the fingers

of two hands clasped together. We can sort out which fingers belong to the left hand and which to the right, but there isn't much doubt about which of those two clasped hands is the upper one. The wild is on the retreat. It survives only by our dispensation.

Don't we act in the service of the wild if we renounce the keeping and killing of domestic animals for meat, if we rid the range of cattle and sheep and return those usurped lands to their rightful owners, the deer and the antelope, the wolf, the coyote, the raccoon, and the bear? And don't we act in the service of the wild, too, if we reassume our place as hunters alongside the wolf and the lynx? Many voices will respond to that question with a resounding "No!" Hunters are obsolete, or ought to be, those voices will say. I would agree that some of the hunters I've met ought to be obsolete. But here in my corner of Maine and elsewhere, there are many hunters I hope will never be obsolete, hunters who have remained, in Wallace Stegner's phrase, "good animals" themselves. They are indispensable to any kind of world I care to live in. They are the ones who know that every wild animal knows far more than they do, who know that a farm animal, deserving as it may be of our care and respect, is an animal of a different order.

The Naskapi hunter eats the boiled ptarmigan with attention and delicacy and care. The grateful hunter turns the tiny bones in his hands and picks every last shred of meat from them, and when he has finished his meal, he hangs those bones in the black spruce tree behind his tent. He has eaten flesh, not butcher cuts, not meat that can be processed and cut up into steaks, roasts, and chops. The comparison to milled lumber–the two-by-fours and two-by-sixes–does not hold for wild food. A ptarmigan is not a factory-farm broiler chicken. The animal hunted and eaten, no matter how hard the hunter has worked for it and "earned" it, remains a gift. The animal raised and slaughtered is not a gift. We have earned that food in a different way, and when we eat that animal, we are not accepting a gift as much as we are exercising our property rights.

Livestock and the meat of livestock can be bought and sold. The flesh of a wild animal can be shared and given away but not sold. We slaughter livestock, but we cannot slaughter a wild animal because we do not own it. It is free until the second it falls dead from the hunter's bullet, arrow, or lance; and even then the hunter knows he does not own the animal. He knows he cannot treat the hide, head, feet, and viscera of the dead animal like offal from a slaughterhouse. In hunting cultures, piety toward the felled prey and its enduring spirit is expressed in innumerable rituals and gestures of atonement and propitiation. Even in our nonhunting, industrialized society, a vestige of that piety remains in our laws and taboos against the buying and selling of birds and animals taken in the hunt. The more practical-minded may object that I should not be stirring law and taboo together here and that laws against trafficking in game were simply straightforward measures originally enacted to curb market hunting. Perhaps. But the shame I still feel for having sold a deer more than forty years ago runs deeper and is totally out of proportion to what has to be regarded, in the annals of the law and of human crime, as a relatively minor transgression.

But even as I struggle to draw distinctions and find reasons for doing what I do, I find I can't entirely trust my own or anyone else's distinctions and reasons. "Man cannot reenter Nature except by temporarily rehabilitating that part of himself which is still an animal," says Ortega. "And this, in turn, can be achieved only by placing himself in relation to another animal. But there is no animal, pure animal, other than the wild one, and the relationship with him is the hunt." That's a mighty pronouncement, one that seems to me, depending on my frame of mind at any given moment, to ring like the gold of immutable truth or to lie flat and flaccid as a slice of baloney. Fine, I'd really love to reenter nature and not just temporarily. And when I look for a way to do that, I find that the hunter-gatherer cultures have the most to teach me. Whatever else their failings, their modes of acquiring food, their social organization, and their systems of belief left the natural world in a state of health and equilibrium that we today can only regard as utopian. So I guess I'd better rehabilitate that part of myself which is still an animal, but then, try as I will, I'm still dragging along that part of me which is not an animal or is at least a mighty impure animal living in an impure world.

Ortega's neat little diagram, his arrow going from man to animal or from animal to man, is much too pat. The word *pure* is almost always suspect. How wild and pure are the raccoons that eat corn and chickens, that raid garbage cans in the village for midnight snacks, that open screen doors, come on inside, and help themselves to the leftover mashed potatoes? How wild and pure are the gray squirrels eating peanuts in Central Park or the Yellowstone bears standing up at car windows to beg hot dogs and Hostess Twinkies? Moose, down to an estimated herd of only two thousand animals in Maine in 1935, have made a spectacular comeback thanks both to a closed season on them from 1935 to 1980 and to the industrial clear-cutting that has decimated the Maine woods. A mature forest puts leaves and twigs out of a moose's reach, but those vast clear-cut acreages coming back in hardwoods anywhere from five to fifteen feet tall make ideal moose cafeterias. So it would appear that the moose, that symbol of the wild North Woods, shares to some extent the ability of opportunistic weed species to thrive on the disasters we human beings have wrought. Our impurity seeps out into the animal world around us.

Our chickens, sheep, and ducks were surely impure, domestic, genetically engineered. Compared with wild animals they were cloddish and helpless. Without human protection and care, they would have perished, as indeed some of them did when I failed to protect them adequately. But for all their impurity and for all the control we humans had over them, they did not—and no domestic animal does—fit perfectly into Ortega's scheme. However much the chicken or sheep may carry our purpose, whether 70 or 83 or 95 percent of its being belongs not to it but to us, it remains to some degree "wild" by virtue of being alive. On some abstract and economic level, my chatter about chattels and cattle and capital may be correct. But for the husbandman who raises and then kills his animals with his own hands, the life of even the most doltish creature escapes those categories. He knows there is an animal other than the pure wild animal; and, his experience tells him, by relating to that impure animal he does rehabilitate some part of himself that is still animal and so reenters nature to some degree.

No matter how deeply we have meddled in the breeding of domestic animals, manipulating this breed of cattle for milk and that one for meat, this breed of sheep for wool and that one for meat, the very fact of life is the wildness that any and every animal retains. The husbandman may be able to control virtually every aspect of his domestic animal's life, including when it will be born and when it will die. But at the moment of slaughter, he will always have to face up to the realization that he can take life but not give it. Religions based in pastoral cultures, like Judaism, built ritual and prayer around the killing of domestic animals, just as hunting cultures did around the killing of wild ones.

Factory farming and mass-production slaughter, which effectively deny life to animals and treat them as biomachinery for the production of meat, milk, and eggs, change the role of husbandman to that of manufacturer of animal products. Because factory farming is strictly about money, about minimizing investment and maximizing profit, its whole impetus is to remove itself as far from nature as it can. It wants maximum predictability and uniformity. The lives of animals in barnyards and pastures are much too unpredictable for the factory farmer.

Small-scale husbandmen know that Ortega's graphic representation of an arrow going from man to animal is an oversimplification. As soon as we take responsibility for an animal, the arrow turns back toward us. On a very basic, physical level, we quickly learn that eggs from range-fed hens have more color and taste better than eggs from battery hens. We learn that meat from range-fed sheep is leaner and better tasting than anything we can buy in the store. Free-ranging domestic animals ingest a bit of the wild and incorporate it into their flesh. Their meat has a gaminess to it that no commercially raised meat has. We learn that a touch of wildness in the diet makes for a touch of wildness in the meat, and that is all to the good.

The touch of wildness has other benefits besides the gustatory. Diseases that plague birds and animals kept in the monocultures of factory farms rarely afflict small, free-ranging flocks and herds. Like human beings, domestic animals seem to find a certain amount of wildness in their circumstances conducive to health and happiness. Can I rightly speak of their happiness? I think so. The alert perkiness of a chicken foraging in the grass attests to chicken happiness. Sheep lying in the shade at noon chewing their cud are not recollecting emotion in tranquillity. They are instead retasting the sweet grasses eaten at daybreak. Sheep, I suspect, process thought and emotion in their four-part stomachs, not their brains; and those slowly moving jaws are telling me that life is good.

What the small husbandman learns from his domestic animals reconnects him to the wild. They form a bridge back into the wild, and if some wild animals prey on his domestic ones, he then has to think about the relation between the two. What accommodations can he make that will both protect his domestic animals and leave the wild ones unharmed? At what point does the keeping of domestic animals begin to threaten the well-being of wild creatures and wild land?

As I've said, we gave up keeping meat animals in response to practical pressures, not because we had thought our way through to any clear position about them. But once we had arrived at that place, it began to dawn on me that if I had a utopian vision, it called for a world where there is ever more room for the wild and where the possibilities for gathering and hunting for food increase rather than decrease. Paradoxically, it was my sheep and chickens that made that vision clear to me.

To say this, however, is not to say I have any illusions, either for myself or for society at large, about returning to a total hunter-gatherer condition, or any desire to. I like my measure of safety as much as the next guy, and a measure of safety is what agriculture gives us. The barrels of potatoes and carrots and beets in the root cellar and the leg of lamb in the freezer are a blessing in themselves and even more a blessing if the hunter comes home empty-handed. And surely the man or woman who personally grows the potatoes and tends and slaughters the sheep is one giant step closer to the gods than the one who never sees a seed germinate or a newborn lamb stumble to its feet. Chances are, too, that the gardener and husbandman will have tasted the difference between a wild strawberry and a cultivated one, between a wild trout and a hatchery trout, between lamb and porcupine. He will know that wildness is the salt that gives the earth its savor, and he will season the life of his crops and animals with it.

IV.

DISH-FED

RETAINERS

If keeping domestic animals for food poses dilemmas, then what possible justification can anyone find for keeping such utterly useless creatures as pets? None at all, plenty of worthy and authoritative folks would say. When we first settled in Maine in 1971, I dutifully read Scott and Helen Nearing's *Living the Good Life*, a book that enjoyed near-scriptural status in the back-to-the-land movement of those days. Scott and Helen were full of excellent advice on how to live a healthy, economically independent life that called for mornings of physically beneficial labor in field and forest and left afternoons free to cultivate the arts and live the life of the mind.

I had not gotten too far into this book before I formed the impression that the Nearings were awfully sure of themselves. Scott, I thought, if some turn in his youth had not led him off the beaten path and onto the byways of leftist politics and rural life, might well have wound up as president of General Motors. He seemed to me to possess the single-mindedness, the drive, the self-righteousness, the obsessive devotion to mission that has made America both great and such a terrible mess.

What I found most irritating about the Nearings, however, was that they were often right, with that kind of schoolmasterly, ex cathedra rightness that inevitably evokes in me a perverse, schoolboyish desire to be as wrong as I possibly can. Actually, I didn't have far to go. The Nearings pointed out, for example, that it was imprudent to buy an old, wood-frame New England farmhouse and try to restore it. No matter how much money and energy you put into it, the building would always be leaky and drafty and in constant need of upkeep; you would be forced to live out your days putting up with all the original builder's design mistakes: the too-small kitchen, the overly large, space-wasting parlor, the upstairs ceilings that were oppressively low. If, on the other hand, you were to build a new stone house, you could design every last detail to suit yourself; the building would be warm in winter, cool in summer, and require only minimal maintenance on such trivia as trim and window frames.

A stone wall was recommended as a garden enclosure instead of some slipshod mess cobbled together out of cedar posts and chicken wire. Farm animals were dirty, expensive, an albatross around your neck, and of course eating either them or any of their by-products—eggs, milk—was bad for you. The wise homesteader would avoid such foods as conscientiously as he would addictive poisons like caffeine and alcohol.

But if there was anything or any creature upon which

the Nearings heaped their most withering scorn, it was dogs and cats. Dogs scared away the wild animals; cats ate the birds; and both of them, the implication was, just ate and ate and dragged fleas and filth into your stone house and shed all over the place and gave you nothing—nothing, mind you—in return. Pets were "dish-fed retainers," a burden on the world's resources.

Now, as I was reading *Living the Good Life* and absorbing all this good advice, I was sitting in a leaky, drafty old New England farmhouse we were in the process of restoring. Evening was coming on, so I put the book down, drained the bourbon-on-the rocks I'd been sipping as I read, put the kettle on for tea, eased the cat off my lap, and took some lamb chops out of the freezer. Then, as I headed out past the garden with its post-and-wire fence to feed and water the sheep and chickens, it finally dawned on me why I felt a nagging sense of incompleteness about our place: We had no dog, and I resolved to correct that deficiency first chance I got.

Since that evening, two dogs have entered and left our lives, and we are now living with Lucy, our third. I have loved all three, but to say merely that I love Lucy would be to say way too little. The love of man for dog and dog for man, as that love is usually understood, is much too platonic, much too companionable and chummy, to even begin to describe what our dog Lucy and I have going. The dog in the classic Lassie, Rin-Tin-Tin scenario is loyal, brave, clever, obedient, adoring. The man is strict but kind. With a firm but gentle hand he exacts well-deserved obedience and loyalty from his brave, clever, adoring companion and chum.

None of that Boy-Scout stuff for Lucy and me. Our relationship has been one of unabashed dithering devotion
from the moment we laid eyes on each other. No sooner
had the attendant at the Franklin County Animal Shelter
ushered Rita, Greg, and me into the kennels than I was
smitten. In that godawful hubbub of yelping, yapping, yipping, barking, leaping, pacing mutts she caught my eye instantly. She had her front paws up against the kennel fence.
She was all black. Her coat was just long enough to have a
slight curl in it; she wore the fringed leggings of a setter or
spaniel; her tail was a great black plume. She was deep-
chested, slim in the loins. And her ears—she had perfect
ears, a bit longer than a Lab's and black and silky but not
those absurdly long cocker ears that the poor little hyper-
bred beasts stumble over and drag in the mud.

Within three seconds, I was ready to sign on the dotted
line, but to maintain at least a semblance of democratic
process and to mask my hopeless crush behind a display of
civilized behavior, I agreed to consider a few other candi-
dates. To give us a little peace and let us get at least super-
ficially acquainted with our possible choices, the attendant
turned us and our few selected dogs out into a large,
fenced-in yard.

Rita and Greg were both drawn to Lucy, too, but unlike
me they had not been blinded by instant unquestioning
love. Every leaning they expressed toward some other dog
I tried to counter with a rational argument and a display of
indifference I hoped would conceal my real intentions and
so not evoke suspicion and resistance. The German-shep-
herd-and-something-else mutt that Rita had taken some

fancy to was, I claimed, too big. His tail was high enough and heavy enough to wipe off the kitchen table with one wag. He would knock little old ladies down and break their bones; we would be sued; he was an obvious menace to our physical and economic well-being.

Greg, who was a savvy sixteen at the time, had his eye on a rough-haired, terrier-looking tyke, a thoroughly unglamourous little mongrel who was so homely he was endearing. Greg is not one to be taken in by fluff and frills and beauty that is only skin-deep. He is drawn instead to characters of real integrity who, though unprepossessing on the outside, remain doggedly true to themselves no matter what, gently defying brainless authority and making their way in the world on a combination of subversive intelligence, spunk, high spirits, and laughter.

"He's too small," I said. "We need a dog big enough to take on long hikes. And I bet he's a yapper. And did you see what he did the minute he got out in the yard? He raced around scarfing up every last bit of shit he could find."

"All dogs eat shit," Greg said.

"Maybe they do," I said, "but he could have been a little more discreet about it. He could have waited until we left."

"I like his honesty," Greg said. "I like how up front he is."

Lucy, meanwhile, had behaved admirably. She had welcomed our attentions but been neither coy nor pushy. She had not barked once. She had shown no interest in poop.

"Well," I said, after ten minutes or so, "I've by no means made up my mind, but that long-eared black female has some good points."

"She looks like a sophomore at Wellesley," Greg said.

"Exactly!" I leapt back. "Young, attractive, intelligent, interested in getting a good education, just the right size, not too big, not too small, looks like a strong swimmer, clearly has some retriever blood, athletic, lively, obviously affectionate, charming, beautiful. . ."

I realized, too late, that I had started to babble.

"I think," Rita said, "we should go home and sleep on it. She is a nice dog, but I like that shorthaired, part-dalmatian, too. He probably wouldn't shed much, and he seems sweet-natured."

"I still like the poop eater," Greg said.

I was in agony. What if, ten minutes after we left to go home and sleep on it, somebody came in and adopted Lucy on the spot? First come, first served was the rule. You couldn't buy an option. You couldn't put money down. Maybe I could bribe the attendant? If I slipped her ten would she lie for me and say someone had already signed for Lucy?

No, no, no. I couldn't do that. Rural Maine is, by and large, still an honorable place. People don't lie and bribe and cheat here. The attendant would horsewhip me out the door. And even if she didn't, how would I–burdened with a Calvinist conscience the size of a woolly mammoth and still unable to forgive myself for the few white lies I've told in my half century plus–how would I ever be able to live with myself if I did something so scurrilous? That such a thought even occurred to me suggests the intensity of my infatuation.

I told myself it was late in the afternoon. Probably nobody else would come in to look at potential adoptees today, and if I called first thing in the morning, if I had that phone ringing at 8 A.M. tomorrow morning when the attendant walked in the door, then probably I'd be okay. Probably, probably, probably. Would I be able to survive sixteen hours of probability? And just as important, would I be able to convince Rita and Greg that Lucy was indeed the dog they too wanted?

Imagined obstacles loom mountainous; the real ones turn out to be mere bumps in the road. At our suppertime dog deliberations, Rita and Greg agreed that if we were going to bring home only one dog and not all the dogs in the shelter, or even the five we had taken a closer look at, then Lucy was the best choice. By eight-thirty the next morning I'd signed the adoption papers and Lucy was on her way to the vet to be spayed. Three days later she was home with us.

She was still very young when we got her—around six months, the vet estimated. That makes her ten years old now, eleven next spring, midsixties, pushing seventy in human terms. Preparations for walks and swims still send her into whirling, wagging tizzies of delight, but she no longer has the staying power of youth. Even two years ago she would still be perky at the end of daylong bushwhacks in Maine's western mountains, still eager at day's end to race after still another red squirrel and bark up his tree. Now an hour's easygoing ramble is more her speed. Where she used to take long, looping forays into the woods ahead of me, always circling back to the dirt road or trail or just my line of travel to check up on me, she now tends to trot along placidly at my heels or, if I decide to jog for a quarter mile or so, even to fall behind. Molly, our neighbors' collie-beagle pup, would wrestle and cavort ceaselessly if Lucy would have it, but she won't. Ten or fifteen minutes of that are enough, and she calls a halt to the horseplay.

Her muzzle is gray; her eyebrows are gray; the fur inside her perfect ears is gray. Rumple those ears, and the silvery gray hair flashes into view. A few years ago, when the gray first started to show, it was the badge of her prime and the full flowering of her beauty, just as the first streaks of gray are in a woman's hair. Now the gray is more prominent; it isn't just an accent in her otherwise totally black coat. Her gray, like mine, is now the mark of late maturity, early dotage, call it what you will—not, I hope, the ultimate chapter in either of our lives but surely the penultimate. Like her people, our dog is eligible for Social Security.

Lucy is a glowing example of just what the Nearings deplored: a useless, mooching creature. She does no work and never did. She doesn't pull a sled, sniff out stashes of dope in airport lockers, or carry shots of brandy to travelers stranded in the snows of the Saint Bernard Pass. (Actually, Saint Bernards don't do that either.) She doesn't herd sheep or point at quail or partridge or retrieve ducks, all activities the Nearings would have deplored, too, examples of depraved humans dragging their already debased dish-fed retainers down a rung or two lower. Had I been keen on upland hunting when we got Lucy, she probably could have learned to be a good bird dog. She has the right genetic makeup. But my interests and focus were elsewhere at the time, and she has remained uneducated as a hunting dog. She eats, sleeps, plays, clowns, schmoozes. She is a pet, and though we may keep pets for companionship, we also keep pets for petting, for the physical warmth, affection, and contact they are almost constantly eager to give and receive. With animals we call pets, petting constitutes a major part of our interaction with them.

In addition to Lucy, we have a hulking tabby cat we call Clunker. I'd be ashamed to say how much of my time I invest in going over him with hands any masseur would envy. If he jumps up on the couch next to me while I'm reading, I start with a couple of strokes on his back, running my hand firmly down the length of him from his neck to the base of his tail, thumb and fingers straddling him, squeezing and pressing just enough to evoke an arching of his back and a look of witless glee on his face. If I scratch his cheeks, he'll lie down and roll over on his back, exposing his chin and throat, the stroking of which soon has him slack-jawed in supine surrender. I move from his throat down to his chest and furry belly. He writhes and opens his mouth in a soundless moan of delight. He stretches his front legs alternately, first left, then right, then left again. His paws spread out wide, and I stick the tip of my index finger into the little pocket that opens between the heel pad and the toe pads. His paw closes, capturing my fingertip in that warm, silken crevice. I cup my hand around the fullness of his belly. He rolls from side to side in flipflopping ecstasy. He is a shameless voluptuary and proud of it.

Lucy does not engage in such brazen displays. Her style has always been more modest; and now, at her advanced age, she is, if anything, more affectionate than ever but not the least bit importunate. Where our neighbors' young dog, Molly, plunks her head in my lap and gazes up at me with eyes desperate for love, Lucy quietly sits down next to my chair and leans her head against my leg. If I gently rumple those perfect ears of hers, she is happy; but she is happy to just sit there too, to just be in touch.

The touching makes us both happy. Petting my cat and dog gives them pleasure, and I take pleasure in petting them. Petting is a manifestation of love for the creature world, and it's one we ache to extend to creatures other than cats and dogs. Stories and legends that link us physically and, often, sexually to animals are legion in every culture. Native American mythologies tell endless stories of the "old time" when humans and animals were much closer than they are now, when people understood animal languages and could talk to all the creatures, when animals could turn into people and people, into animals. People mate with bears, rattlesnakes, owls, and, interestingly enough, even with dogs. These marriages are not trouble-free and end-lessly blissful any more or less often than marriages between humans are, but they attest to a kinship in which human and animal cohabit in every sense of that word, sharing both hearth and bed, and they suggest to me how much we humans want to affiliate with the animal world, not just metaphorically but in the flesh. The "caribou man" of the Montagnais and Naskapi lives among the caribou, eats caribou moss, sires caribou, yet is not a caribou. The animals allow him to kill some of their number and use their skins for his clothing; they sleep close to him at night to keep him warm. He is both of them and not of them, and it is he who dispenses caribou to the deserving among his human brethren, denying them to hunters who disobey the law by killing more than they need and wasting food.

If the human–dog bond originated in a hunting partnership, then it would seem that from some very early time in human history the dog has been involved in our primary economic activities. Predators ourselves, we joined forces with a fellow predator whose vastly better nose and ears and much faster legs made him a great help to us in the hunt. Then, by genetic engineering, we produced ever more specialized hunters: pointers, terriers, hounds, retrievers. When we became herdsmen instead of hunters, we started using dogs to guard our domestic animals rather than hunt wild ones; and here, too, we introduced specialization, breeding dogs that became primarily guard dogs or herding dogs. It is not surprising that over those centuries of working relationships bonds of affection and trust developed between humans and dogs. Bonds created by working together at basic life-sustaining tasks are among the strongest bonds there are.

But the most radical step in the human–dog relationship has been a by-product of industrialization and the industrialization of agriculture and animal husbandry. For anyone who sees humankind's evolution from hunter-gatherer to agro-industrialist as unmitigated disaster for both humans and the natural world, the genetic engineering of the dog from wild canid to the many highly specialized breeds we have today is bound to appear as a parallel disaster. If the step from hunter to herdsman-plowman was the first great step in the process of alienation from nature and self, then surely the step from herdsman-plowman to city dweller, driver of combines, and feedlot engineer has all but completed that process. We still have hunting dogs, and we still have herding dogs, but we have vastly more companion dogs.

As we human beings have retreated more and more from the wild world ourselves, we have bred more and more wildness out of some dogs until they have been almost totally stripped of their animality. Lapdogs and toy breeds have been so drastically engineered away from their wild origins that about the only role they could assume in the wild would be as prey, not as predators. They haven't legs enough for either pursuit or flight. They haven't teeth or jaws enough to kill, scavenge, or defend themselves. Like pointers or border collies, lapdogs too have been bred for a special purpose: not to hunt or herd, however, but to be petted and coddled.

Over the past few decades the late Paul Shepard wrote about such matters, deploring the awful fix we human beings got ourselves and the rest of all creation into when we gave up the hunting and gathering life to raise crops and keep domestic animals. The degraded creature I see in the coddled toy, however, Shepard sees in any and every domestic animal—"the mindless drabs of the sheep flock, the udder-dragging, hypertrophied cow, the psychopathic racehorse, and the infantilized dog." For him, my amiable, easygoing mutt is every bit as much a neurotic "protoplasmic farrago of dismantled and reassembled life" as any lapdog:

> *[Dogs'] relationship to us is not symbiotic, either,*
> *or mutual or parasitic. None of these biological*

*terms is suitable to describe organic disintegration
in a special vassalage among creatures whose heart-
warming compliance and truly therapeutic presence
mask the sink of their biological deformity and the
urgency of our need for other life.*

*Less than kindly euphemisms for "companion
animals" come to mind–crutches in a crippled society, candy bars, substitutes for necessary and nurtu-
rant others of the earth, not simply simulations but
overrefined, bereft of truly curative potency, peons in
the miasma of domesticated ecosystems.*

Well! I think, with no little indignation, Paul Shepard
may be able to get away with saying nasty things like that
about lapdogs, but he can't say them about *all* dogs. Lucy
is no candy bar or peon. No lapdog this, no ludicrous little
Chihuahua or Pekingese or shih tzu that a coyote could
make one mouthful of. *My* dog is a sturdy, noble mutt who
can run and swim for miles, chase red squirrels up trees
and bark wildly and gleefully about her accomplishments,
flop down in the shade and snooze and hang out with me
contentedly, even if I'm doing all those dumb things people
do that aren't any fun for dogs at all: splitting and piling
wood, reading, writing, shingling roofs, weeding gardens.

But rejoice as I will that my dog is indeed a cheerful all-
American and not an overbred freak, I still have to recognize that in many respects she can't measure up to her
wild cousins. When I see coyotes whirling off across the
snow like wisps of snow in the wind themselves or when I
watch the precise, purposeful economy of the red fox's en-

ergy-saving trot and see the luxuriant magnificence of his red tail flowing behind him, I know I'm looking at beasts of a different order. The memory I have of a pack of wolves running along the bank of the Grand River in Labrador, those great, lean creatures striding out with a grace and power that seemed to practically lift them off the earth into skimming flight, how they materialized out of nowhere, leapt silently along beside our canoes for a few hundred yards, then disappeared again up over the bank, when I remember that, I gasp all over again with wonder, admiration, amazement at the glory of those animals. My dog, much as I love her and delight in her, cannot compare with them. When we are out rambling together and I see her trotting along with her tongue hanging out in her big grin, her head and tail up, the bounce and lilt of her gait as her black-fringed legs flip the miles out behind her, I grin too. She is fun; she is charming; but she lacks the high seriousness of the wolf. Her tracks in the snow belie her. Where the wild canid moves with care and intent, Lucy travels in extravagant, wasteful loops and sorties. Where she is sweet and clinging and a little clownish, the wolf is independent, self-contained. It has a kind of stature no dog can match.

Konrad Lorenz gives lower marks to the spaniels and long-eared gun dogs than to the huskies, chows, and German shepherds, which are of wolf lineage. Lorenz allows that setters and other longhaired, long-eared breeds are affectionate but, for his taste, affectionate to a fault. Too "sentimental," he calls them, affectionate to the point of fawning. They lack the spunk, feistiness, and independence of the more wolflike dogs. The drooping ears and short skull base that the setters and spaniels retain throughout life occur in wild canids only in their early development and disappear in the wild adult. But then all dogs, in their dependence on their human masters, remain "childlike" to a greater or lesser degree throughout their lives. "It is a remarkable fact," Lorenz writes, "that a dog, which fits into human society better than any other domestic animal, owes its major behavioral characteristic to neoteny . . . ; just like actively investigative openness to surroundings in human beings, fidelity to a master represents a persistent juvenile characteristic in the dog."

Lucy is clearly of long-eared, gun-dog lineage, and she is just as clearly sentimental and soulful. But then I'm soulful and sentimental myself. Maybe that's why we get on so well. I know she lacks the wild grandeur of a wolf, coyote, or fox, but then I lack the wild grandeur of a Masai or Apache hunter. In his sentence about neoteny, Lorenz is saying, in somewhat arcane language, that Lucy and I, each in our own distinctively canine and human ways, have just never quite grown up. Her fidelity to and dependence on me and my "actively investigative openness to surroundings" (read: childlike curiosity about the world and wide-eyed fascination with it) are persistent juvenile characteristics. Lucy's seemingly wasteful circling and sniffing is the image of the human mind actively investigating its surroundings, often randomly, often barking up the wrong tree. That both of us have the luxury of squandering our energy this way is, depending on how you look at it, either a benefit or a curse of domestication.

The idea underlying Paul Shepard's trenchant attack

on our keeping and breeding of any and all domestic animals—indeed, the single informing idea in all his work—is that the development of human intelligence is inextricably linked to the separation of nature and culture and to the hunter's consequent attention to animals "not as stuff or friends but as resplendent, diverse beings, signs that integrity and beauty are inherent in the givenness of the world." Conversely, the blurring of the line between nature and culture, the consignment of some genetically engineered animals to our laps, the milking barn, and the slaughterhouse, and the concomitant withdrawal of our attention from wild animals all bring about impoverishment in both our internal and external worlds. With "nothing but our own image to explain ourselves by" and our gods created in our own image, the only reference point that matters is the human one. We spin about in ever diminishing circles of selfhood, as the bookstore shelves sagging with self-help so eloquently testify. In our narcissism, we try to squeeze all external reality inside those same little circles with us.

The force of Shepard's argument is compelling. As the human population grows and grows and as our destruction and domestication of wildlife habitat continues to drive increasing numbers of wild creatures into extinction, it is hard to resist the idea that our agro-urban world with its overpopulations of humans and domestic animals is destroying the integrity and beauty of the given world. When I go into my local supermarket and see an entire aisle taken up with pet foods, I too can see all those cans and boxes and bags as evidence that we are investing vast amounts of energy and resources in maintaining the "wrong" animals. But still, I leave the store with my twenty-five-pound bag of Dog Krunchies, and though I find the case Paul Shepard makes elegant and persuasive, the nature–culture division underlying it remains, as Shepard himself says, "merely methodological." His argument seems a bit like a small-scale planimetric map that provides the overview necessary for seeing where we are in the world and in relation to our ultimate destination. But for day-to-day travel, we need large-scale topo maps that show us the bogs and tiny brooks, the mountains, cliffs, and canyons.

What Shepard's map tells us is that we have stumbled so deep into settled, domesticated territory that we have lost touch almost completely with the wild world and so with the wellsprings of our own mental and physical health, and on his map we can see the direction we need to go to get out of that fix. But for today's journey, I need the large-scale map of my immediate surroundings, too; and on that map, the companionship of my dog, my affection for her, her affection for me, and the heavy petting I bestow on her all loom large.

If we have sinned by overindulgence in pets, then our sin–like so many of our sins–is one of degree, not kind. We are not sinners by virtue of our being tool makers. We are sinners only in having made too many tools that are too dangerous and destructive and in using them so recklessly. If we have bred physical and psychic flaws into dogs and if we have let their populations displace wild creatures, the sin is in our excesses. If farm animals are a link to the natural world, then dogs and cats are an even stronger one. They are—or at least can be—at once both "wilder" and "more domestic" than cattle; they range and forage, are capable of greater independence from us, but are the only animals that share our living quarters. Like us, they are creatures of both the hunt and the hearth. To say that there are too many of them and too many of us and that together we make excessive demands on our world's resources is not to say that either they or we are intrinsically evil. If only it were as easy to right the balance as it is to make that grand observation.

But whatever the big picture, the small picture of my life includes a bond with Lucy so strong I suppose it borders on lunacy. Even to my mind, which is not adept at logic, my affection for Lucy seems illogical. How can I insist on the grandeur and wonder of the wolf and still value, no, not just value, but love my dog, who is not as grand and wondrous? Have I no rigor, no standards?

A recently divorced friend of mine said of her ex-husband, "Oh, he's charming all right, but charm is not a cardinal virtue." Mary Oliver, in her wonderful diatribe against that revolting Disney vision that would make all of nature a petting zoo, writes, "Nothing in the forest is charming. . . . And nothing in the forest is cute." All things in the forest and we humans too are, again in her words, "wild, valorous, amazing."

"Humans or tigers, tigers or tiger lilies—note their differences and still how alike they are!" How different Lucy and the wolf are and still how alike. How different the old Naskapi hunter and I—yet still, I hope, at least a little bit alike. How impossible for Lucy and me to extract ourselves from the muddled past of our species and be anything but the part-wild, part-tame beasts we arè. No wonder I love her. She is both of me and not of me. She partakes of my confusions. She is a messenger from the world of fur and fang I can not only reach out and touch but also live with and hold close. Her eye may never have harbored the "fierce green light" Aldo Leopold saw die in the eyes of the she-wolf he shot in Arizona, but in her youth Lucy was a beautiful creature, capable of great grace, of bounding valorous leaps; and even though that beauty and valor are muted now in her declining years, she still charges out into the world with an animal vitality that has its origins much farther back than any human interference with her genetic makeup. Her being is not exhausted in her domesticity and charm. She may be "my" dog; I may, officially, have the power of life and death over her. But beyond all officialdom she is her own self, and when she snuffles and pounces in the tall grass in pursuit of rodents or rolls on her back in the snow, squirming in sensuous abandon, what she's telling me is this: "I may love you, man, and you may love me, and we may both like the hearth rug, but out here is where the real action is. Don't you forget it."

And because I love her dearly, I take to heart everything she says.

V.

CONTEXT NORTH:
HUNTING ALL THE TIME

We get off the train about ten-thirty at night. The stop is Menihek Dam in north-central Labrador. The month is February; temperature, about twenty-five below zero. The diesel engines roar, and the train slowly rolls away, taking our bubble of warmth with it and leaving us and all our gear—toboggans, duffels, boxes of food, day packs, tents, stoves—scattered trackside where we have hastily unloaded it and ourselves from the baggage car. I've come along on a winter trip led by my friends Alexandra and Garrett Conover, who own and operate North Woods Ways guiding service based in Maine. Over the next two weeks we will make a loop through the Menihek hills to the west of us, up one watershed to Howell Lake, over a not very high height-of-land, down another watershed to Pointer Lake, up a third, down a fourth valley, and back to Menihek Lake, where we are starting.

But all that is yet to come, and tonight is tonight. Our disembarking is a lucky one. The sky is so flawlessly clear that half a moon is quite enough to give us all the light we need, the air so motionless it creates an illusion of warmth. I have the fleeting, nutty idea that it would be fun to strip down and moonbathe out here on this beach of snow, in this soft, still air.

Instead, we set to work loading the toboggans, lashing the loads down. We'll haul about a mile up the shore, past the railroad embankment, and make camp there.

The air may feel mild, but twenty-five below is still twenty-five below. I've had my mittens off too long; my fingers are behaving like ten torpid snails as I tie the last few knots on my lash lines; and by the time we're packed up and ready to move, the wires between brain and fingers have just about gone down completely. When I tell my fingers to bend, to pick up the loose end of a lash line and thread it under a running line on the toboggan, they obey but only slowly, sluggishly, stiffly. I couldn't pick up a dime off a tabletop. I couldn't tie another knot.

"My hands are gone," I say to Alexandra.

"Put them on my neck," she says.

Inside her hood is an oasis of body heat. In a few minutes the desired agony of rewarming begins, and after a few more minutes I can stuff my hands back in my mittens and let the warming that comes with getting under way take over.

The way of the northern winter is a constant hunt for heat, a hunt so constant and so imperative that it becomes second nature. Hunting is so inextricably woven into living that the hunter may momentarily forget that he is hunting and think all he is doing is snowshoeing across an open bay, but he is also looking across the bay for the sheltered cove, the thick little copse of black spruce where he can shelter out of the wind to wolf down some crackers, cheese, salami, peanut butter, fruitcake, and hot tea, stoke up his internal furnace. With that charge of food inside him, he gets moving again before he starts to chill down. As the afternoon wears on, he starts hunting for the night's camp. Again, he wants to be out of the wind; he wants plenty of standing deadwood to fuel his stove. The fuel his lunch gave him is just about all gone, and he won't be hauling a toboggan anymore today. His heat won't come from inside him now, so he'll need to find some outside.

He sets up the tent and stove, cuts and splits his wood, lights his fire. Wood is food for the gut of the stove; the stove digests that food and radiates heat that fills the fragile membrane of the tent, making another tiny oasis of warmth. The comfort of the tent marks the conclusion of another successful hunt, even though no bird or animal may have been shot. The hunt for heat is unending, the hunt for food to sustain us and warm us from within, the hunt for wood to warm us from without. We borrow the heat from dead spruce, from ptarmigan, caribou, geese, ducks, lake trout. We borrow it from under a companion's hood.

꧁

A year and a month later, Garrett and I are pounding our way across Attikamagen Lake east of Schefferville, Quebec, following Garrett's Naskapi friend, Daniel Walker, to a camp Daniel has set up on one of the long arms of this huge lake. The wind has packed the snow into hard ridges, and our snowmobiles slap down over them like canoes bucking heavy waves–kathunk, kathunk, kathunk. The constant jarring keeps shaking loose the two five-gallon gas containers lashed to the back of my komatik, and I have to stop, think how I will lash them on this time so they won't come off, retie them, set off again, look back in five minutes, and see them bouncing along behind me again like tin cans tied to a dog's tail.

The day is sunny and bright, but the northwest wind is so strong that it is still tearing spindrift up off this snow that seems hard as concrete underfoot. Daniel has no komatik and speeds on ahead, leading the way. Garrett, looking back, sees me stop, and he stops. I retie the containers again and set off after the snow-beclouded figure in front of me. On something like the fourth try, I devise a system of loops and knots that finally holds, and we progress uninterrupted into this bitterly cold, fiercely exhilarating afternoon.

Daniel's camp is tucked in on a lee shore; the shelter is the usual Naskapi structure that looks something like a loaf of bread about seven or eight feet high but with sloping sides and not much pitch to the roof, a frame of black spruce poles with big tarps stretched over them. It's three o'clock, and since Daniel wants to be back at the Naskapi settlement before nightfall, all he does here is gas up his snowmobile and head for home.

Garrett and I have come to Schefferville expecting to spend a few weeks in the bush with Daniel and his wife, Mary. The original plan was for the four of us to head another thirty miles or so north from this camp on Attikamagen to a lake where Daniel, as a young man, had spent many winters before the iron mines and the railroad came to Schefferville; indeed, before there was a Schefferville and before anyone had ever dreamed of skimming along on top of the snow on little gasoline-powered sleds. But Mary has had to go to Sept Isles for some medical appointments, and it is unclear when she will return. Daniel will come back out in another couple of days, with her if she is home, but in any case to check a few traps he has in the area.

Ordinarily, Alexandra would be along on this trip, too, but she has decided to spend these weeks with her family in Massachusetts instead. As for my family, Greg is off at his second year in college, and neither he nor Rita has ever been keen on making subarctic trips, whether winter or summer. So Garrett and I are on our own.

We set up our tent and stove; cut, saw, and split firewood; chisel a hole through the ice for water; and because we expect to be here for a few days, we take the time to lay a luxurious spruce-bough floor in the tent. By six in the evening we are ready to crawl inside, hang up our moccasins and mittens, and cook. The makings of tonight's meal come from the supermarket in Dover-Foxcroft, Maine: rice, a little bannock, a couple of small steaks that thaw out fast. Daniel gave us a big hunk of frozen caribou haunch, but chopping it up into usable form is another chore we don't want to deal with tonight.

We spend the next morning settling in. I cut, saw, and split enough firewood to hold us for two days or so. Garrett resharpens the ice chisel he bunged up yesterday when the first water hole he cut was too close to shore. In a place where ice is routinely three and four feet thick and rocky shorelines slope out gradually to deeper water, it's easy to misjudge and find rocks instead of water at the bottom of a water hole. Encounters with rocks dull the soft edge of the chisel and reduce the efficiency of the tool by something like 30 to 50 percent. That reduction translates in turn into a corresponding increase in the time and effort needed to cut the next hole. By contrast, a keen, flawless edge on the chisel gives the hunter an edge in the metabolism game, that perpetual, ongoing process of balancing caloric income against caloric outlay.

We'll want that edge this morning because we're going to start hunting fish with set lines today, and for each line we set, we will have to cut a hole through those three or four feet of ice. Before Daniel left yesterday, he told us the most productive water was about a hundred yards offshore from camp and we should set our lines out there in a row parallel to the shore. We go to work, taking turns at the tiring job of chipping our way down to water. Maximum result with minimum effort calls not only for a razor-sharp chisel but also for an optimum strategy. From years of chopping holes in the ice, Garrett knows vertical strokes that practically blast big chunks of ice out are more efficient than angled ones, and he knows that about thirty-five strokes are needed to go once around the perimeter of a twelve- to fourteen-inch hole and break up the crown of ice left in the middle. Any more strokes just chop the ice into smaller pieces, making it harder to clean out the hole with a slush scoop. Garrett speculates that the vertical strokes work best because they follow the "verticality" of the crystalline formation evident in the candle ice of spring when the ice breaks up. As in splitting wood, so in splitting ice: Working with the grain produces maximum results with minimum effort.

Once we have broken through and the water comes gushing up in the hole, we make our set. Daniel has given us not only a hunk of frozen caribou to eat but also some strips of red sucker for baiting our fishhooks. We thread a strip onto a hook nearly four inches long, a monster the mere sight of which could make any Catskill trout fisherman used to fishing dry flies tied on tiny little No. 18, 20, 22, and 24 hooks faint dead away. But for the fish we are after–lake trout and pike of five, seven, ten pounds or more–these hooks are the perfect tool; so too is the forty-pound-test line that we tie to a small spruce stripped of all its branches but a small tuft at the tip for visibility and planted at an angle over the hole in the ice. The butt is driven down into the pile of slush and ice chips we've scooped out of the hole, and in a matter of minutes it will freeze solid there.

I doubt that any sport fisherman would look at this rig of spruce pole, heavy line, monster hook, and red-sucker bait and allow that it had anything to do with angling as he knows it. But if you look at our rig from an etymological perspective, we are as much "anglers" as the guy with the split-bamboo fly rod, for we too are fishing with a hook, which is to say an *angle*, a word whose trail can be traced back through Middle English to Old English to Latin *uncus* to Greek *onkos*, meaning "barbed hook." But etymology be damned. We and the Catskill fly fisherman know better. We know that we are fishing, not angling. We may be using a hook, but we are not pursuing sport; we're pursuing meat.

"Fishermen" use huge hooks and heavy set lines; they use nets, weirs, and spears. Fishermen are out to gather food. If Daniel were still with us, we might well be setting gill nets under the ice now, unlikely as that very idea may seem. How can anyone set nets under the ice? In the water, you set gill nets by anchoring one end of the net, running the rest of the net out behind a boat, and then anchoring the other end. The principle is the same in winter, but the system is different. You cut holes as far apart as your net is long. You fasten one end of the net to a pole that will reach to the farther hole, then run the pole and net to the farther hole, pull out the pole, and anchor the net at both ends. Or if the net is longer than any manageable pole can reach, you cut several holes and pass the net from one to the other until you have it stretched out full length. Granted, it's a cold, arduous process, but if you calculate the odds against our set lines, the investment is worth it. The yield from a well-placed net is likely to be much greater than that from even a whole long string of set lines. And if laying in a food supply is what fishing is all about, if fishing is not angling but another form of food hunting, then whatever tools and techniques promise the greatest yield in the shortest time with the least expenditure of effort will be the preferred ones. Alaskan poet John Haines, for example, writes of food gathering with a hook that is not a fishhook but a gaffhook:

> *Standing here, watching the ice come down, I re-*
> *call past years when I came to a channel much like*

this one, in mid-October with only an inch or two of snow on the gravel bars, to fish for salmon. I had with me a long pole with a steel hook at one end. Standing very still and quiet where the current slackened against the ice, I watched for the glowing red and pink forms of salmon on their way upriver in the last run of the season. Sometimes I caught sight of one toward mid-channel, beyond reach of my pole; but often they traveled slowly along the edge of the ice, finning and resting, at times nearly motionless in the current. And carefully I extended my gaffhook along the ice edge behind the fish, and with a sudden, strong sweep and jerk I struck the fish through its body and flung it ashore.

The big hook made a nasty gash in the side of the salmon, and fish blood soon stained the snow where I piled them, one by one. If the fish happened to be a female heavy with eggs, the eggs sometimes spilled through the torn side of the fish, to lie pink and golden in the shallow snow with the glazed, mottled bodies of the freezing salmon.

There was something grand and barbaric in that essential, repeated act. To stand there in the snow and cold air toward the end of the year, with a long hook poised above the ice-filled river, was to feel oneself part of something so old that its origin was lost in the sundown of many winters: a feeling intensified, made rich by the smell of ice and cold fish-slime, by the steely color of the winter sky, and the white snow stained with the redness of the salmon: the

*color of death and the color of winter. And to all this
was added the strong black of the ravens that gathered each evening as I was leaving the river, to clean
the snow of the spilled eggs and blood.*

*I caught the big fish one at a time, watching and
walking quietly along the edge of the ice, hour after
hour. In a few days I had from two to three hundred
salmon heaped in scattered mounds in the thin, dry
snow of the sandbar, to be packed home a few at a
time, heavy and frozen.*

Our standard term *hunter-gatherer* rightly suggests
that hunter-gatherer people engage in both activities, but
the term also suggests that hunting and gathering are sep-
arate and distinct. The term conjures up images of men
going out to stalk deer and bring them down with arrows
while the women are gathering berries and nuts and dig-
ging up roots. But when the salmon make their fall run up
the river and John Haines hooks them out of the water and
piles up two or three hundred of them, he may be fishing,
but he is also gathering in the fruit of a predictable natural
crop just as much as if he were gathering ripe blueberries
in August. When Daniel Walker pulls his nets and picks the
fish out of the mesh, he too is as much gatherer as hunter,
plucking fruit from an underwater tree, and when Garrett
and I return to these set lines we are putting out, we will
gather in the fish that have taken our baits.

Trapping—whether setting nets or lines underwater to
catch fish or setting snares for snowshoe hares—is a food-
gathering activity somewhere between hunting and gath-

ering. Like the hunter, the trapper has to know the ways of the creatures he means to trap, but in the taking of what has come into his traps, he is a gatherer. For people who truly live off the land, the distinction between animal and vegetable food, between hunting and gathering, is moot, and Paul Shepard suggests *foraging* as an inclusive term. Food exists on a continuum. The Inuit hunter who kills a seal and eats it is also a gatherer who harvests the sea-weeds in the seal's stomach and eats them. To hunt is to gather, and to gather is to hunt. Both constitute what one does to live.

❦

It's about three in the afternoon by the time Garrett and I have set three lines, and we head out to use what daylight is left hunting ptarmigan. As we approached camp yester-day, we cruised close to shore to look for tracks in the wil-low flats, and just a quarter to a half mile south of camp we saw enough tracks to lure us back there. Where there is smoke there is usually fire, but where there are tracks there isn't necessarily game. We push back in from shore among the black spruce, sinking knee-deep in the powder snow despite our snowshoes, but find no birds.

No birds, but as we swing back to camp, we check the set lines and haul up one good-sized lake trout. I kill it right away with the little spruce club we have along for that purpose; back in the tent, we slice the fish into steaks and put them in a pot to boil.

We pass two days hunting the willow flats near camp,

checking the set lines, puttering, eating, talking. Daniel returns on the third day but only to check his traps. He still has no definitive word from Mary. We make bannock in his camp and eat lunch together; he goes out for an hour on his snowmobile and comes back with one marten, then heads for home.

On the afternoon of our fourth day we head north about ten miles onto the stream that flows into Attikamagen Lake from Cormier and Gulch Lakes, and just where the stream comes out of the last of three little ponds in the river we come onto a big flock of ptarmigan. We want to shoot simultaneously, hoping to both get doubles, but Garrett is ready before I am.

"They're getting nervous," he whispers. "I've gotta shoot now, or I'll miss my double."

I'm still pulling my gun out of its case, and I say, "Go ahead."

He shoots; two birds crumple; he reloads, fires again, and a third drops. The flock rises up, flies a hundred yards upstream, and settles again. While Garrett is plucking and drawing his birds, I slowly walk up within range. The ptarmigan are too widely scattered for me to get more than one in my shot pattern, so I pick the closest single bird and shoot it. The flock again lifts off and flies upstream, this time out of sight.

Garrett draws up next to me on his snowmobile and says, "I'll run upstream and see if I can pick up a couple more."

I nod and start plucking my bird. If you pluck them immediately, within five minutes of the kill, the feathers come out easily and the bird's still-warm body lessens the risk of frostbitten fingers on bitterly cold days. I pluck the body clean, cut off the wings and legs at the first joint, cut off the head close to the body, peel off the crop, cut a smile-shaped incision below the keel, reach inside to pinch off and pull out the intestines below the heart, lungs, and liver, cut the anus free, and lop off the pope's nose. The wings make perfect soft, white towels to clean the blood off my hands.

This method of cleaning ptarmigan saves everything edible on these small birds. Not all ptarmigan hunters are as saving and respectful as the old-timers who clean their birds this way. Some hunters tear just the plump breasts out of the birds and throw the rest away. I've seen hunters in Maine do the same thing with partridge, a practice reminiscent—on a smaller scale, perhaps, but in principle the same—of buffalo and caribou hunters cutting the tongues out of thousands of animals and leaving the carcasses to rot.

Garrett is back in a few minutes. The flock has disappeared upstream, and we have enough birds for a couple of suppers, so we turn back toward camp. As we are just emerging from the brushy shoreline onto the lake, I fall off the snowmobile trail Garrett is cutting in the snow ahead of me. I'm a novice on a snowmobile, and I lack the combination of balance, snow sense, and machine sense it takes to keep one afloat and moving forward on deep powder. I tilt to the left; the left ski nose-dives, rolls the machine over on its side, and dumps me into three or four feet of fluff. I half-wallow, half-swim back to the machine, put on my snowshoes, and start packing a ramp for the snowmobile to climb back up on and punching the snow down on the right side of the machine so I'll have something firm to roll it up on. I've been through this process a few times before already in these, my first few days of extended snowmobile travel. I've learned that this is a job worth doing slowly and well the first time so I won't have to do it again when a poorly prepared attempt ends in more foundering and wallowing.

As I plod and pack my way around the machine, I hear Garrett's 12-gauge boom once, then once more—two more birds, one more supper for us. On this little afternoon foray Garrett has shot five ptarmigan to my one. His skills in everything we have done this afternoon are more highly developed than mine. His vision—which has less to do with keenness of eyesight than with a learned ability to register and correctly interpret every bit of information his eyes show him—enabled him to spot that first flock of birds before I did. One morning he pointed toward the base of a black spruce about thirty yards away and said, "There's a ptarmigan." I couldn't see anything but snow. A ptarmigan in winter plumage is, after all, white, white as snow, but Garrett had spotted the bird's black eye.

And then there is his familiarity and fluidity with his over-and-under rifle-shotgun. He was loaded and ready to shoot before I had my gun off my back; he didn't miss a shot; and on our way back to camp, he saw and shot two more birds because he had the skill on his snowmobile to stay on top of the snow where he had his eyes free to see more game and his hands free to shoot it, all while I was spending my time bailing myself out of a hole.

To hunt successfully requires a whole repertoire of skills, one in which handling the snowmobile well is crucial because you can neither see nor shoot game if you're half buried in a snowbank. In the North you're hunting all the time; you never stop hunting. Hunting is living, and living is hunting. If you do something dumb–something that may not be intrinsically catastrophic but that interferes with the constant attention and awareness essential to hunting and, hence, to life–then you may miss chances to gather some food. Competence in northern life means never missing any of those chances or at least missing as few as possible. And utterly consistent with that definition is never wasting ammunition and never shooting if the odds for a quick, clean kill are not strongly in your favor. In this context wingshooting makes no sense. Indeed, for the food hunter, wingshooting rarely if ever makes sense. Why risk a miss, a wasted shell, a wounded bird, the loss of food, when shooting a sitting bird all but guarantees instant death for the ptarmigan, duck, or goose and a sure meal for the hunter? In this context the sporting ethic, indeed the very concept of sport, seems alien and out of place, as much an odd and impossible import as a palm tree in a clump of black spruce. Which is not to say, of course, that this "unsporting" mode of hunting is not "fun," if the word *fun* can even begin to encompass the endless fascination of hunting all the time, of hunting not as an entertainment but as a mode of being in the world.

*

In the evening, with a couple of candles lighting the tent and two ptarmigan and some rice boiling in the pots, we remark how totally absorbing this life is, these days taken up wholly with just the business of living—well, almost wholly. We do have a few books along, and we turn to them after we've eaten and cleaned up at night. I'm struggling with an introductory Russian grammar, preparing for a semester Rita and I will spend in Russia as exchange teachers; Garrett is learning Cree syllabics, and before we turn in one or the other of us reads aloud a story from a volume of Kundera short stories. But the books and reading are peripheral at best, and we find ourselves wondering if we would miss them at all if this life were the life we lived all the time. In my "real" life, of course, just the opposite is true. I spend most of my time in a world of books, words, reading, translating, and writing. At home the hunting, fishing, and woodcutting, the birding and botanizing, the seemingly aimless daily rambles somewhere along Temple Stream or on the hill back of the house, the engagement with what grows and runs and flies outside my bookish world—all those things come second, not first. But important a second as they are, so important that what I do first would dry up and die without them, they are still second in the sense that I earn most of my bread with the words and the books.

When the ptarmigan are ready and we begin feasting on that wild, dark meat, picking every last tiny bone clean in hungry gratitude, nothing beyond the joy of this food and this warm tent seems, for the moment, to matter much. How well does the genius of Kundera stand up next to the genius of the willow ptarmigan with its feathered feet and legs and its three molts a year? Where will the Parthenon or Goethe's *Faust* or Dante's *Divine Comedy* come out in the final wash? Puzzling over why cecropia and promethea moths keep their cocoons off the ground while the cocoons of the pale green luna moth and the polyphemus moth are found in the leaf litter, biologist Bernd Heinrich writes: "As in all living things, each creature does it its own way, and very small, perhaps almost random selective pressures may start a cascade in one direction that, once started, continues on its own momentum to ever greater differentiation and perfection. Not a shred of intelligence is needed to make it, nor to make it work. It is strange to me that life itself doesn't strike the average person as all that impressive, but for some reason 'intelligent' life does. When you consider life as a whole, intelligence is a mere bristle on the hog."

Privileged as I am, living most of my life in my exquisite little valley in western Maine where I wake up every morning with more of the hog than I will ever begin even to see, much less comprehend, right in front of me, I still spend a disproportionately large amount of time preoccupied with that mere bristle. And depending on your point of view, the constructs of human intelligence–books–that absorb so much of my working life may be the ones closest to the hog and most revealing of it or the ones most remote from it. What could be more abstract, airy, and unhoggish than words, and what human endeavor could have less to do with hog life as a whole than trying to arrange those abstract, airy little symbols into patterns of ever greater differentiation and perfection? And yet it is often those patterns–the poems of a Mary Oliver or the prose of a Barry Lopez or Bernd Heinrich–that lead us back from our man-made, manufactured world to life as a whole, both to its vast scope and to its most intricate minutiae.

What do you think? I ask Garrett, returning to a question that fascinates me endlessly but that I know I will not have life or time enough to answer: What if this were the whole of our lives, this life we're living right now, just the hunting, the fishing, the daily rounds of finding food, wood, water, and shelter? I find it so completely satisfying that I imagine I could walk away from 95 percent of the things I do at home and never miss them at all. How important would our highly elaborate arts and sciences seem in a life where the science of observing and knowing plants and animals was directly linked to day-to-day survival, where the making of efficient tools, clothing, and shelter was essential to survival, where song, story, and dance all celebrated the ties to the plant and creature life that made survival possible?

In my imaginings, this life would become even more satisfying and engaging as our skills and knowledge increased and our dependence on what we have brought with us lessened. Eventually our sheet-steel stove would burn out; our wool clothes, our luxurious Egyptian cotton tent, our brilliantly designed and sewn wind gear, made of that same high-count cotton, would wear out. Sooner still, we would run out of ammunition for our versatile combination rifle-shotguns that let us carry only one firearm but give us the capabilities of two. And much sooner still we would run out of gas for the snowmobiles, which would then become utterly useless hunks of metal and plastic abandoned on some lonely lakeshore. More and more of our time would have to go into making implements and clothing. This afternoon's twenty-mile round trip to bring home six ptarmigan would not be a matter of a few hours but of a day or more. In the context of a real subsistence life, we never would have undertaken it; the little bit of lean meat we have brought home would in no way have justified the expenditure of our own energy to obtain it. But because petroleum and the internal-combustion engine did most of our work for us, we were able to spend a pleasant afternoon that has left us comfortably tired but not exhausted and to bring back some delicious, nourishing food that feeds us in some way beyond our purely physiological needs but without which we would not have gone hungry for even one night, much less starved.

We are not complete dodos kidding ourselves into thinking we are competent to live off this land. We have a pretty clear idea of how vastly ignorant we are and how much we would have to learn—preferably slowly over several years and not in a crash course that would most likely kill us—to become competent. We know that our safety and comfort out here depend not only on what we know and know how to do but also on what we have brought with us: the axes, the saws, the stainless-steel cooking pots, the *chandelles "Radiant"* made in Saint-Constant, Quebec, the whole outfit right down to the needles and thread and whetstone and epoxy in the repair kit, not to mention enough food to see us through even if we never caught a single fish or shot a single ptarmigan.

Our outfit is an umbilical cord back to the world of industry and agriculture; it is our deep-sea diver's air line.

Without the big ship that has not only supplied the raw materials of our gear—the cotton, the wool, the iron ore—but has also fashioned those materials into clothing, axes, guns, matches, not to mention flour, baking powder, bacon, and sausage, we would be lost. (The Cloud Nine Espresso Bean chocolate bar isn't crucial, but it is nice.) If we were truly to live out here without benefit of our industrial aids, we would need skills and crafts we don't have; we would need knowledge of animal behavior and migrations we don't have; we would need the help of mates, parents, brothers and sisters, aunts, uncles, and cousins; we would need to know things we don't even know we don't know.

In his 1920 book *Labrador* William Cabot writes about his attempts to shoot mergansers from the bow of a canoe on the Peribonca River in Quebec. Whenever Cabot and his Native companion got within easy range, the birds would duck under so quickly that Cabot missed every shot. Exasperated by this display of incompetence, the Indian steersman turned the canoe around and, pursuing the ducks again, slapped the water with his paddle every time a bird surfaced, making it dive before it could get its breath. In this way the Indian exhausted the ducks and was eventually able to kill most of them by hitting them with his paddle. How many members of Ducks Unlimited would ever dream of (a) taking ducks with a canoe paddle and (b) eating a merganser?

If we failed to find caribou where we thought we would find them, we could not just jump on our snowmobiles and run fifty or sixty miles north or south to look for them. Without firearms, we could not even think of hunting as we think of it now. We could not reach out across 100 or 200 or 250 yards to take a single animal. We would have to think, as the Naskapi used to, about spearing large crops of migrating caribou at places like the narrows of Mistinipi Lake.

Finally, of course, we have to realize that in asking ourselves how well and happily we would adapt to a totally pre-industrial hunter-gatherer life we are not asking, as we were fond of saying in my college days in the 1950s, an existial question. We are not and will not become pre-snowmobile, prefirearm Naskapi hunters. And no matter how deep our belief that the hunting life—which is not a life that just includes a hunting trip now and then but a life that is constantly finding means of sustenance in the land one inhabits—is a rich and satisfying life and one conducive to modest and respectful living, we are rooted in the world that made us, tied to it by myriad connections, human and otherwise, devotees of disciplines and pursuits we have no desire to give up. Bernd Heinrich is surely right about intelligence being a mere bristle on the hog, but that mere bristle is our distinctively human bristle. And even though the segment of it that has occupied so much of my life—the curious business of trying to find out what I think by putting words down on paper and by reading what other people have put down—may well be just a tiny piece of a tiny part of the whole hog, it is nonetheless still part of the hog and therefore crucial to it, for a hog without bristles can hardly be called a hog at all.

So our question isn't how do we become pre-industrial hunter-gatherers, which would require us to tear ourselves in half and throw away the half that still lives in Maine and does all the things we do there. The question is not how do we tear ourselves apart but rather, how do we put ourselves back together? How do we reconcile the hunter with the writer, the moviegoer, the shopper at Shaw's supermarket? Is it not absurd for us to go out and kill more food if we have duffels with enough food in them? And beyond that, what are we looking for up here in Labrador if the life we have in Maine is—on so many levels and in so many ways—as rich and satisfying as it in fact is?

*

We're in Labrador because the reach of the human empire is not so strong here. In this context, the legitimacy of the hunt is not in question because the prevalence of the wild is still so clear, because the only food this environment yields in sufficient quantity to sustain life is food obtained through the hunt. Only in the North have I ever experienced firsthand those "comminglings of outer world and inner flesh" that Richard Nelson finds in northern hunter-gatherer cultures, that interplay of human and animal, that almost osmotic process in which the elements of the human and natural world flow back and forth like gases or fluids between cells.

The far northern reaches of Quebec and Labrador are, on the one hand, sparse, barren, and empty: As you move ever farther north, passing the fiftieth parallel and heading toward the sixtieth, you encounter first the thinning boreal forest, then the stunted black spruce and caribou moss of the taiga, and, finally, the glacier-scoured rock, the willow and dwarf birch. Go far enough north along the eastern shore of Hudson Bay and up into the Ungava Peninsula, and you're in a place all water and sky and the bare bones of the earth. Here, it's easy to imagine the earth in its infancy, what the world must have looked like before God got around to inventing plants and animals. The scale is macrocosmic, and the only vegetation all this rock seems willing to tolerate even now, after how many millions of years of evolution, is diminutive and microcosmic, a dense matting of tiny, ground-hugging plants. Everything you see is too large, too remote, too rock-hard to ingest or digest, or it is too small and too poor in nutrients to sustain life. Even if the prolific cloudberries were ripe all year round and not just for a few weeks in summer, man cannot live from cloudberries alone. Vegetarianism is just not an option in the Arctic and subarctic, and what vegetable foods are available are acquired by "hunting," that is, by gathering. The farther north one goes, the less hospitable the soils and climate are to any kind of agriculture.

But, on the other hand, this land that can seem so empty and devoid of nourishment, too naked even to satisfy the birdlike appetites of its white-crowned sparrows and horned larks, can also be downright profligate with creature life. In summer brook trout and lake trout, plentiful and huge, hurl themselves at flies and spoons so recklessly that they hook themselves not just in the mouth but in the eye, throat, fin, and tail as well. It is a mistake to say, when blessed with this kind of abundance, "I am catching fish." Accurate as that statement may be on the face of it, it gives far more credit to the fisherman than is his due. He is not

the successful pursuer of prey so much as he is the fortu-
nate receiver of a gift. He is not "catching" these fish; they
are coming to him like manna from heaven.

And there are the caribou. Their tracks and trails are
everywhere in summer, but day after day there are no animals to be seen. Then one day they too are everywhere,
appearing out of nowhere. You are windbound, sitting for
your third day straight as wind out of the west keeps re-
lentlessly hammering the long reaches of some huge lake
into heaving, unnavigable mountains of water. You look up
from your book and there across the little cove from your
camp is a caribou. And as you look, you see not just one
caribou but two, then three, then half a dozen and a dozen.
And beyond that dozen just across the little cove are perhaps fifteen or twenty more on the hillside. And when you
get out your binoculars and start scanning every hill in
view, you see they are everywhere, far and near. If you turn
around and walk the hundred yards or so to the other side
of the point you're on, you can look across a mile of water
to the next point and see them crawling like ants on the
hillsides there and silhouetted against the skyline.

At night you hear their ankle joints clicking as they
move past your camp; you hear their teeth tearing up food.
At breakfast the next morning they are grazing peacefully
all around you like a herd of cows. If you walk toward
them, you can get within thirty, twenty, sometimes even fifteen yards before they will start, trot off a few yards, then
stop to turn and look at you, their huge racks poking up
into the sky. And when the wind finally lets you go, and
you start traveling northeast, threading your way through

the islands, coves, peninsulas, the caribou accompany you, plunging into the water in herds of twenty and thirty and eighty to swim unerringly on a course they need no compass or map to hold to. Sometimes there will be a lone animal pushing across a mile or two of open water. Why is this herd animal alone, and where is it going? An idle question, of course, because, to quote Richard Nelson's Koyukon mentor again, "Every animal knows way more than you do." Maybe I don't know why that lone caribou is crossing a big bay in Lake Minto all by itself, but it does.

For the subsistence hunter, these caribou would be like the fish: a gift, manna from heaven–a gift both expected and unexpected, however, for the subsistence hunter would know from years of his own experience and of his ancestors' experience where he should be and when he should be there to receive this gift. His knowledge would be wide, deep, and practical, knowledge gained from his people's centuries of observing weather patterns, seasonal changes, the movements and behavior of all the creatures in their native territory. But he would know the limits of practical knowledge, too. He would know that no matter how wide and deep our practical knowledge is, it may not be wide and deep enough. So he would attend to dream and augury as well, and he would maintain a courteous and grateful spirit appreciative of past gifts received and humble in the awareness that they could be withheld at any time in the future.

So if anyone else asks me or if I ask myself why I go north to Quebec and Labrador, that is surely part of the answer: to partake as best I can of that commingling of outer flesh and inner world, of inner flesh and outer world, still possible where hunting and fishing remain major sources of food and where most local hunters hunt without a trace of sentimentality but with a matter-of-fact respect for the creatures they kill and eat, creatures of which they can truly say, "This is my body; this is my blood."

Notice how Daniel Walker eats. He wastes no scrap of meat from the tiny ptarmigan. He picks each bone absolutely clean; when the meal is over he does not toss the bones into the stove or out onto the snow to be trampled underfoot. He takes them outside the tent and hangs them in the branches of a spruce tree.

These gestures of respect are not accompanied by any grand pronouncements, rituals, invocations of gods, or hoisting of chalices. They strike me not so much as religious gestures whose meaning has to be constantly reaffirmed but rather as acts of simple courtesy based in an order so ancient and taken for granted that the acts are sufficient in themselves. Because flesh and soul, animal and human, have never been torn apart in this tradition, there is no need to loudly proclaim their unity.

Down here in our lower forty-eight, formidable obstacles stand in the way of experiencing that kind of connection with a landscape and its creatures, a connection whose nature the metaphor of osmosis so aptly captures. Here the relevant metaphor is not osmosis but the map overlay, that device cartographers and geographers use to isolate features on the landscape. In the beginning was the world, but now we see it on paper and through plastic. On one overlay we draw in roads; on the next, buildings; on the next, agricultural lands; on the next, state and national parks; on the next, timber holdings. When we're all done, we can still see the original contours and features of the earth, the mountains, rivers, and streams, but they are all several layers down, not immediately present to the eye but filtered; no matter how transparent those transparencies are, the world beneath them is still at a remove, twice, thrice, and more removed, remote, tantalizing because we can see it but no longer touch it.

The overlays and imprints of human activity on the land are often so massive that we can only guess what this land was like in its natural state, and when we alter landscapes radically, the animals in those landscapes then take on roles and definitions we give them, sometimes intentionally, sometimes unintentionally. In parts of Wisconsin, for example, deer have become so numerous that they are called "corn rats." Without the suppression of the deer population that hunting provides, depredation by deer could put some Wisconsin farmers out of business. For hunters, those deer may be game animals and sources of food; but for the farmers whose crops the deer decimate, the deer have become vermin—corn rats indeed—in the dictionary sense that they compete with humans for food. So Wisconsin hunters and Wisconsin deer are both cast in peculiar dual roles: Those deer remain one of North America's highly valued game animals yet are at the same time rats, and those who pursue the deer are, on the one hand, hunters and, on the other, exterminators of an agricultural pest.

On Texas game ranches, where hunters pay substantial fees to hunt whitetails, the deer are not a threat to the rancher's income but a highly desirable and profitable supplement to it. Under the best of ranch management regimens, the deer and their environment are manipulated to protect vegetation and other wildlife, to promote the health of the deer themselves, and to produce trophy animals for the clientele. Though these deer remain wild as individuals, they are collectively as domestic a herd as any herd of cattle with which they share their range. A well-managed game ranch yields many undeniable benefits: It is good for the land, good for wildlife, good for its owners, good for the local economy. Still, the almost total subordination of wild animals to human purposes raises the question of where the wild animal ends and the domestic one begins, of just how much management we can impose on wildlife before it ceases to be wild, of how controlled the circumstances of hunting and fishing can be before they cease to be hunting and fishing. As Aldo Leopold put it years ago in his succinct way: "Very intensive management of game or fish lowers the unit value of the trophy by artificializing it."

Vastly more artificial than even the most tightly controlled herd of white-tailed deer, however, are the Asian axis deer, the Indian blackbuck antelope, and other exotic beasts offered up as prey at some Texas game ranches. Try as one will to find a redeeming rationale for these enterprises—the economic benefit to ranchers who might otherwise fail financially and have to subdivide and sell their land, the preservation of some species dying out in their native countries–the arguments against them carry far more weight. Most wildlife biologists look askance at exotics, troubled by the possibility of these animals transmitting to native species diseases as exotic as themselves and by the ability of some exotics, like sitka deer, to outcompete whitetails. And then, apart from these issues of species health and ecological equilibrium, there are the social and ethical issues. No matter how large the acreage enclosed by the fence of a game ranch and how fair the chase within those confines, it's hard to think of a hunt under such circumstances as anything but potting a zebra or oryx in an oversized open-air zoo. Perhaps nowhere is the disconnect between hunter, prey, and landscape more blatant than on these game ranches for exotics.

Here in rural Maine, dissonances in the relationships of hunter, prey, and landscape are not as pronounced as in those Wisconsin and Texas examples. Large blocks of woodland surround our fields and little villages, softening and sanding and rounding the sharp angles and edges of land cut up to fit human designs. Here, deer are neither rats nor cows; their numbers are not large enough to make them pests, though residents of some suburban areas in southern Maine may disagree. Of course we have, and have to have, wildlife management, but animal populations across an entire state cannot be as tightly controlled as the population of a game ranch under single ownership. Our only major game species imported from another continent is the brown trout. Here, numerous as our map overlays are and heavy as humankind's managerial hand has often been, there are still wild and ragged patches and edges left over;

and in them, we who live here are privileged to experience some inkling of that seamless unity that land, hunter, and hunted retain in the world's remaining wild regions.

At its best our landscape is lovely in its blend of nature and culture and a terrain with which I am irrevocably in love. But even as I confess to that love, I'm mindful of Wallace Stegner's remark: "In gaining the lovely and usable, we have given up the incomparable." It is that loss that haunts us as hunters and, I think, not just as hunters. Because our hunt is not essential to survival, it lacks ultimate seriousness. And even though more of us hunters say we hunt primarily for food rather than for sport, that declaration in no way changes the fact that we will not starve if we fail to bring home some wild meat. At some level the game we pursue inevitably remains just that: game. It's a curiosity of our language that the generic term under which amusements as various as football and Parcheesi are subsumed is the same term we apply to animals we hunt.

But more than that accident of language, it is our economy and land-use patterns that marginalize hunting, fishing, and foraging, making hobbies of them. If we obtain most of our sustenance from lands that we alter drastically to produce our man-made foods—not to mention the alterations we make by extracting coal and oil and timber, building cities and highways, and so on and on—then those uses of land will become primary, and our oldest use of land as a source of wild foods will be demoted to secondary status. We come first; our plans come first; the earth's and animals' plans have to come second. What is left over after we've done our real work, we can use for play.

And what, one can reasonably and legitimately ask, is really so different about the Canadian North whose wild integrity I've been praising so lavishly? Quebec and Labrador have their fish and game laws, too. They have their licenses, their caribou tags, their fisheries and wildlife biologists, their game wardens. They have their bush pilots and guides and outfitters who, for about the same amount of money you'd spend to shoot an oryx in Texas, will put you onto some classy trout water or set you down where a caribou will wander into your gunsights. They have their gargantuan hydroelectric projects, their iron mines. The differences between the unroaded, unsettled, unpeopled North and Maine—or Connecticut, for that matter—are differences only of degree, not kind. In vast tracts of the North, the hand of man the manager may not yet have been felt, but there is no place on this globe that is free of his purview. A helicopter can land just about anywhere. Today's wild river is tomorrow's hydroelectric impoundment.

So, the cynical and even not so cynical might say, those of us who make our two- or three- or six-week sorties into the Far North must be kidding ourselves. What we experience up there is just a Potemkin wilderness. In Maine lakefronts and riverbanks are required by law to have buffers of uncut woods to shield boaters' eyes from the devastation industrial forestry has wrought behind those beauty strips. Push back through the few yards of uncut land along the renowned and legendary Allagash River, and you'll find yourself face to face with the wreckage of the Maine woods. In Labrador or the Northwest Territories, the cynical might say, the beauty strip is just a bit bigger, not fifty or a hundred yards but fifty or a hundred or a thousand miles. But behind that beauty strip, no matter how wide or narrow, lies the real world, which is intent on chewing away at the beauty strip until all creation has been converted from the incomparable to the usable; then, all too often, the next step is to use the usable up, leaving nothing but the useless behind.

Indeed, the cynical might say, not only you people who go up there and paddle your canoes or run around on snowshoes for a few weeks each year but even the Native people in their villages are living let's-pretend lives. Granted, they are out hunting and fishing much of the year and deriving a significant amount of their food from the land, but if they did not hunt, they would not starve. The daily plane will still keep the co-ops in the remotest Arctic and subarctic villages supplied with flour and sugar, potato chips and Coke. Is it not absurd to think that people who run around all winter on snowmobiles and all summer on ATVs and whose baseboard heating and electric ranges and TV sets run on electricity generated by fossil fuels are keeping the old ways alive?

But however "impure" those of us are who make our pilgrimages to the North, however much we remain tourists and outsiders from the industrialized world, and however much the Natives of those regions have been drawn into our orbit, what they and we still experience there—in a landscape still largely free of overlays and among animals still largely free of human purpose and definition, animals that are neither vermin nor game nor cattle nor trophies—what we experience there is, quite simply, what remains of the balance and order that prevailed on this planet for millennia before man assumed the role of Lord Man.

How "spiritual" this experience is, each of us will figure out according to his or her own lights and leanings. For my own prosaic self, I can claim no revelations, visions, epiphanies. I know only the truth I can see and hear and touch and smell. There may well be and doubtless is a larger truth behind the surface truth, but those surface truths are truth enough for me. What is more mundane and quotidian than the cutting and splitting of wood, the acquiring and preparing and eating of food? But then what is more miraculous than the heat of the fire, the transfer of the animal's heat and energy to us, the savor of meat in the mouth, the glow of meat in the belly? In the North, where the shadow of Lord Man rarely falls, the land and its creatures are luminous with life given, and so one lives there in a state of ferocious happiness. That is why I go north–to touch and taste and see.

❧

It is August. Our canoe company of eight is camped at Big Point on Labrador's Lake Winokapau, where men and women have camped since time out of mind. We cut alders, lash them together, and build a dome-shaped frame. We secure tarps over the frame, dig a small pit in the sand in the middle of our little lodge, lay a carpet of alder twigs all around the pit. We gather many stones, none much larger than a cantaloupe. We pile them together and heap all the driftwood we can find on them.

Come evening, we light the fire. When the wood has burned down, the rocks are glowing red, a small volcano in the fading light. With a heavy forked stick we carry some of them, one by one, into the lodge and put them in the pit. We strip, crawl into the lodge, and, with a spruce whisk, sprinkle water onto the glowing rocks. What rises off the rocks is not steam but a vapor so fine it is invisible; then, as it quickly fills the low dome of the lodge, it descends, engulfing us in a wave of damp heat so intense we gasp for breath and feel a momentary, suffocating panic that quickly gives way to euphoric languor. Sweat pours off us. We sip water. The heat penetrates skin, muscle, lung, gut, bone.

Finally, someone opens the flap, and under a pale blue sky brightening with stars and a half-moon, we wade out into the lake, flop down into the water.

Twice more we recharge the pit with fresh rocks from the volcanic pile, sit in the heat, sweat, cool off in the lake.

For the last cycle, only four of us are left. We sprinkle the glowing rocks. "Again," someone says. And "Again" and "Again."

The air is so dense and hot that we kneel with our heads down on the ground, searching for remnants of cooling air. This is the limit of what we can stand, I think, but once again momentary fear gives way to exhilaration. We are breathing an air so charged with heat and water that we blossom like hothouse plants.

A Brule Sioux legend tells how the sweat lodge came into being. A young maiden lived with her five brothers who went out to hunt every day. Then, one day, only four of them came back; the next day, only three; then two; then one; then none. In despair, the maiden tried to kill herself by swallowing a stone, but instead of dying, she became pregnant. She gave birth to a son, whom she named Iyan Hokshi, or Stone Boy. The boy grew ten times faster than ordinary children, and his mother knew he must have unusual powers.

When he was old enough to go hunting, she told him how his five uncles had disappeared and begged him not to go hunting. But he promised to return and bring her brothers back alive.

On his hunt, Stone Boy came upon a ramshackle tepee where an old hag lived. She invited him in to eat and spend the night. When she asked him to massage her back, he felt something sharp and guessed that it was a poison knife or spear, so he jumped up and down on the hag's back until he had broken it and killed her.

In the tepee were five bundles that Stone Boy thought must be his uncles, but he did not know how to bring them back to life. When he went outside, he found that the gray, round stones in a heap there were talking to him and that he could understand them. They told him to build a domed hut out of bent willow sticks and the hag's buffalo robes. Then he heated the stones red hot in a fire. He took them and the hag's water bag into the hut and set the five bundles around the inside of the hut. As he sprinkled the stones with water, he felt stirrings around him; he opened the hut flap, closed it again, and sprinkled the stones a second, then a third time. After he sprinkled the stones for the fourth time, the desiccated bundles began to talk and sing.

When Stone Boy opened the flap for the last time, the

moonlight and the light from the fire outside streamed in, and he could see five healthy young men sitting with him in the lodge.

"This little lodge," Stone Boy said to them, "these rocks, the water, the fire—these are sacred, these we will use from now on as we have done here for the first time: for purification, for life, for *wichosani*, for health. All this has been given to us so that we may live. We shall be a tribe."

In the sweat lodge (or the Russian banya or the Finnish sauna) earth, air, fire, and water are fused in a *spiritus*, a breath that we in turn can breathe in. You'd think the ancient Greeks, who thought all matter was made up of those four elements, would have been great adherents of the sweat lodge, too. Empedocles thought that where strife prevailed, the elements were separated; where love prevailed, they were joined. In this imperfect world we usually find only partial minglings. A hot spring is a blending of only fire and water; a volcano, a blending of earth and fire. In the sweat lodge, stone drenched in fire vaporizes water and makes it air. The sweat lodge may be one of the few places we can experience a blending of all four elements. But it was not anywhere in the outside world, Empedocles thought, that the four elements were held in their most nearly perfect mixture and balance; it was in our blood. And so, Empedocles thought, we human beings think not with our brains but with our blood.

We modern folk may know better. We may know about brains and neurons and synapses and such, but our language and experience know better yet. We know the difference between hot-blooded and cold-blooded. We know that the heart and blood leap and race. Blood is the medium of thought imbued with feeling. Bloodless thinking is spiritless thinking. It's no fun.

To talk this way is, I know, to wallow in metaphor. But how can anybody possibly talk about the sweat lodge without wallowing in metaphor? Metaphor is what we get when blood thinks, and when blood, which is after all one-quarter stone, starts thinking, it can hear its blood brothers the stones talking. And if blood does what the stones tell it to do and brings the stones of earth together with fire, water, and air, then what happens in the sweat lodge or sauna is a meeting and exchange between the elements inside us and outside us, a commingling of outer world and inner flesh.

I do not mean to appropriate, or misappropriate, the Sioux legend. I can't claim Tunka, the Sioux stone god, as one of my gods, nor can I claim that any religious revelations of either a Native American or Nordic variety have come to me in the sweat lodge or sauna. I've never been transformed, transmuted, transmogrified, purified, beatified, sublimed, or sublimated. What I have experienced, however, is an apotheosis of physical pleasure so intense and all-encompassing that it does indeed set the blood to thinking. Anything that feels this good, my blood says, bloody well must be sacred. Stone Boy knew what he was talking about. The sweat lodge is a creation metaphor. The dome of the lodge is the sky. We sit in a circle, north, south, east, west. The glowing rocks at the center are at once the hot core of the earth and the heat of the sun. The damp heat brings dry, desiccated earth to life.

In the lodge we meet cosmic forces on a microcosmic level we can tolerate. The heat is intense but not so intense we catch on fire; the air is drenched with water but not so drenched that we drown. In the lodge we feel the power of the elements to destroy us but also their life-giving power. We breathe damp air in and we pour perspiration back out. In that transpiration we experience the constant interchange of energy that is the hunter's life: the taking of heat and energy from the animal, the expenditure of heat and energy in the hunt.

And from the womb of the lodge the tribe is in fact born. Stone Boy had that right too. In the lodge we are made siblings. We emerge from it naked and wet, brother and sister.

So who needs revelation if you've got all this? Stone Boy had it right, and so did Empedocles. Just listen to your blood thinking, and it'll tell you most everything you need to know.

VI.

FOOD, SPORT, AND
WILD HUSBANDRY

I think I could turn and live with animals, they are so
  placid and self-contained;
I stand and look at them long and long.
They do not sweat and whine about their condition;
They do not lie awake in the dark and weep for
  their sins;
They do not make me sick discussing their duty
  to God;
Not one is dissatisfied—not one is demented with the
  mania of owning things;
Not one kneels to another, nor to his kind that lived
  thousands of years ago;
Not one is respectable or industrious over the
  whole earth.
            WALT WHITMAN, *Song of Myself*

Ah, yes. Who would not like to turn and live with animals? The wolf does not lie awake in the dark and weep for

the caribou it has brought down. The caribou does not sweat and whine because it is prey for the wolf. It's just we humans who fret and fuss. Ortega tells us that to hunt is to reenter nature by temporarily rehabilitating that part of ourselves which is still an animal, but he also acknowledges that a hint of criminal suspicion clawing at our consciences will be the price we will have to pay. If we try to turn and live with animals as animals ourselves, we will not achieve that placid, self-contained state Whitman yearns for. And though we may not lie awake weeping for our sins, we will surely wonder if we have sinned because we well-fed folks here in the so-called first world know that agriculture and the local supermarket have relieved us of the need to hunt and forage for survival.

But that practical point, it seems to me, is not what weighs heaviest on us. In her essay "Sister Turtle," Mary Oliver notes that though she has eaten almost no meat for some years, she does still occasionally crave it.

> *. . . to consider Nature without this appetite–this other-creature-consuming appetite–is to look with shut eyes upon the miraculous interchange that makes things work–that causes one thing to nurture another–that creates the future out of the past. Still, in my personal life, I am often stricken with a wish to be beyond all that. I am burdened with anxiety. Anxiety for the lamb with his bitter future, anxiety for my own body, and, not least, anxiety for my own soul. You can fool a lot of yourself but you can't fool the soul. That worrier.*

I've always liked to think that members of hunter-gatherer societies are untroubled by this particular anxiety and do not question their other-creature-consuming appetite. They have to play by the rules; they have to abide by established ritual and do nothing to offend the spirits of their prey. They have to handle the meat, hides, viscera, and bones with the proper respect; and if they fail in any of these duties, they might suffer the consequences, such as a scarcity of game or, in the worst case, starvation. But the legitimacy of the hunt itself is not in question. One can be a moral or immoral hunter, but one never has to ask whether hunting is moral or not. As long as the hunter-gatherer abides by the established codes, he will have the force of tradition, of community approval, and of religious sanctions to support him.

The Judeo-Christian tradition is a pastoral tradition, not a hunting one. We may have religious prescriptions for killing the fatted calf but not for hunting the wild caribou. Because hunting has never been a primary source of our food throughout our recorded history, we western European peoples have never developed religious sanctions for the hunt. So both as individuals and as a society, we keep worrying the issue. Ortega tells us we have not achieved ethical perfection in hunting. Of course we haven't. Even though we may keep telling ourselves "Thou shalt not kill" is supposed to apply only to other human beings, we can't help taking it as a blanket proscription. So deeply ingrained is that commandment, whether we call ourselves Buddhist, Christian, Jew, agnostic, atheist, or pagan, that our worrying souls question the killing of anything that walks, swims, or crawls; and sometimes we even worry about killing plants.

"William," Hayden Carruth writes, in one of his "Faxes to William,"

> *William, I hate fishing. I hate to kill.*
> *Killing even a nearly brainless pike or a*
> *totally brainless broccoli unnerves me. I long*
> *to come to nature not as an intruder killing*
> *and ravaging but as a compleat insider, one*
> *of the fraternity, paid up and at my ease*
> *forever. But I hate to kill. William, how*
> *can we be friends? How can I be a poet?*

Carruth is not alone; we all hate to kill, even those of us most convinced that pursuing and killing wild animals is not only a morally justifiable way of acquiring food but also one of the most important ways humans can acquire citizenship in the natural world. Unlike the wolf, who is a compleat insider and one of the fraternity, we are not paid up. We are not at our ease forever. We live lives of unending confusion and contradiction. One minute we are expending considerable effort to kill an animal; the next, we are going to sometimes ridiculous lengths not to kill one.

I always check the bathtub before I turn on the shower to make sure there are no spiders in it. If there are any, I carefully lift them out and send them on their way. And if, in one of my frequent moments of abstraction, I forget to check for spiders and then see one swirl down the drain in the first deluge of water, I feel criminally negligent, not guilty of murder, I suppose, but surely of spiderslaughter, a felony in any case, good for ten years with maybe a chance at parole after five.

Just a few weeks ago I was bringing my winter's firewood in from the outdoor drying shed to the wood room in the house. As I lifted one stick off the pile, I exposed a female deer mouse suckling three young in a nest she had made there. I carefully repiled the wood around her and left off my work, hoping that she would lead or carry her brood elsewhere in the course of the night. When I resumed my wood moving the next day, the mice were in fact gone. What their fate was in the intervening twenty-four hours I cannot know. Maybe they made it safely to some new nesting place. Maybe they became a meal for an owl, a fox, a weasel. But either way, it was not I who left them without a roof over their heads, exposing them to their enemies or to the frost of the October night.

A few days earlier still, while driving home in a pounding rain, I saw a painted turtle making its way across the road. At the first driveway I came to I turned around, went back, parked on the side of the road with emergency blinkers flashing, bailed out of the car, and ran down the middle of the road toward an approaching pickup truck, my hand raised for the driver to stop. He did. I picked the turtle up, raised it in both hands like a chalice for the man to see. He grinned and gave me a thumbs-up.

I was drenched. I hadn't taken the time to pull on a rain jacket. Wallowing into the brush a few paces on the side of the road the turtle had been heading for, I was about to just set it down when I had sense enough to look closely at it. It was drawn into its shell, so I could get only a hint of the pattern on the head, but the shell itself and that beautiful red lacework the painted turtle has around the rim of its carapace was far more gorgeous than I remembered it. No pope, no king ever wore anything as splendid.

But still, I wondered as I climbed back into my car, am I not nuts, getting soaked to the skin and running into the teeth of oncoming pickup trucks to save a small turtle from being squashed when, in every season of the year, I'm out in the woods and on the waterways trying to kill and eat creatures every bit as beautiful?

Savior of spiders, mice, and turtles in distress. Sometime killer of deer, partridge, ptarmigan, salmon, bass, trout, sunfish. I don't make any sense, but then again maybe I do. When I kill an animal to eat or cut down a tree to build the fire that warms me, I feel regret at ending a life that I've come to think is, in its own terms, every bit as rich and full as my own. But at the same time I feel grateful for these gifts of food and fuel and blessed by the wild world that has given them to me. Powerful as my sense of blessedness and gratitude is, however, it is not clear and pure, not free of ambiguity and question. I can't untangle regret from celebration.

Blessedness is neither a word nor a state that our language or cultural traditions usually associate with hunting or hunters. The Lord, we've been told for centuries, is not a hunter but a shepherd. Blessed are the meek, the merciful, and the peacemakers, not the hunters. And so, blessed as I may feel when I have received the gift of a wild creature's flesh, that blessedness is tainted with blasphemy.

How can a killer dare to speak of blessedness as he slits the belly of the fish open, tears out gills, pectoral fins, heart, liver, guts, swim bladder with one yank, runs his thumb up under the backbone to peel away the chamber of blood there, and already the bright stippling of the skin is fading? What kind of brute can be happy that he has reduced this brilliant, vibrant creature to a handful of guts, a puddle of blood, a pound or two of edible flesh?

We do cut the fisherman a little slack, of course, because Simon Peter, Andrew, James, and John were fishermen, and Jesus said he would make them fishers of men, clearly a nobler calling than being fishers of fish, but still, catching and eating fish must have been okay or Jesus never would have multiplied two poor little fish into a meal for five thousand people. Then, too, much of Izaak Walton's *Compleat Angler* is taken up with Piscator's effort to woo Venator away from the crass sport of hunting and convert him to the more contemplative and holy enterprise of angling; and in the course of his argument Piscator cites one pious churchman after another, starting with the disciples, who were devotees of this far gentler art.

Also, quite apart from the benefits fishermen enjoy as latter-day disciples, many people who balk at killing and eating mammals have few or no reservations about killing and eating fish. Fish are cold-blooded. They do not copulate. The female lays eggs; the male fertilizes them with his milt. Birds are another story: They are warm-blooded, and they do copulate. But the development of the embryo takes place outside the mother's body, and she does not suckle her young. Killing a bird is worse than killing a fish, but it is not as bad as killing a mammal. Mammals are much too much like us. Look at the raccoon's hands, the deer's soulful eyes. Male and female mate in a passion akin to ours. The mother carries and suckles her young.

And so we have developed a hierarchy of animal killers that casts the killers of fish as gentler souls than the killers of birds and the killers of birds as gentler, or at least more gentlemanly, than the killers of mammals. Bird hunters carry double-barreled shotguns with elegantly checkered stocks and inlaid receivers depicting English setters on point and pheasants flushing. Their weapons have a very limited effective range; for an upland shotgunner fifty yards is a long shot. In the evening bird hunters sit around the fireplace in a well-appointed lodge and drink single-malt whiskey. Deer hunters carry unfancy, high-powered rifles that, like army rifles, can kill a human as well as a deer at two hundred and many more yards. I would wager that the term *slob hunter* is applied more often to deer hunters than to bird hunters, and *slob fisherman* is a term rarely heard, no matter how deserving of it a given fisherman may happen to be.

So even if I can scrape together a case for my blessedness as a fisherman, trying to convince myself or anyone else that I am blessed when I'm pulling the guts out of a dead deer is a tougher sell. I want clarity and redemption. I'm sick of ambiguity and my constant irresolvable internal tug of war, those two teams of huge workhorses pulling away at the Magdeburg hemispheres, straining and straining and unable to pop them apart. The vacuum created by wanting to kill and hating to kill is too strong. And maybe it is so strong that even hunter-gatherer cultures were not and are not entirely free of it either. Perhaps their prayers and rituals to appease the gods and to keep the spirits of the caribou, the salmon, the bear, friendly are evidence that they could not be utterly certain of anything either, except that they knew, clearly, as we do not, that they depended on the health of the biosphere for their survival. Isn't every ptarmigan bone hung in a spruce tree the hunter's way of saying, at least in part, "Lord, I believe; help thou mine unbelief"?

But I can't just adopt the ways of hunting peoples and feel I'm getting off scot-free. What is a perfectly legitimate gesture for a Native hunter, like hanging ptarmigan bones in a tree, seems false and pretentious for me, a misappropriation of a tradition and a piety I have no right to claim as my own. On the other hand, how else can we create a respectful bond with the creature world except by deliberate acts that may initially seem alien even to those of us performing them and insisting upon them? Perhaps all ritual is false, empty, and pretentious until, through constant practice, we fill it with meaning. As Luke Ripley in Andre Dubus's "A Father's Story" says, ". . . ritual allows those who cannot will themselves out of the secular to perform the spiritual, as dancing allows the tongue-tied man a ceremony of love."

A couple of years ago, when I was hunting with a friend who is one of the finest hunters I know—and *fine* means here skillful, successful, knowledgeable, and ethical—I heard him shoot twice about a quarter to half a mile away from me. By the time I had reached him, he had just about finished dressing his deer out, and he had also erected a small shrine of spruce twigs as a gesture of respect and of gratitude for the gift of food he had received. He made no touchy-feely pronouncements or fuss over this simple, straightforward acknowledgment of his debt to the creature world.

He would no doubt object if I called this gesture of his a religious one, but I'll risk his objection and call it a religious gesture anyway, one that acknowledges both the celebration and the regret we feel at inflicting the deaths that sustain our own lives. In her "Sister Turtle" essay Mary Oliver quotes Teilhard de Chardin's remark that "man's most agonizing spiritual dilemma is his necessity for food, with its unavoidable attachment to suffering." Even the most skillful and ethical of hunters has to acknowledge that unavoidable attachment. Try as he will to kill cleanly and swiftly, he will sometimes fail. Instead of dropping the deer with one perfectly placed shot to the heart, he smashes the shoulder and has to pursue the hobbling, wounded creature until he can kill it five minutes later, maybe twenty minutes later, maybe even longer. Worse still, he may wound the animal and never recover it. He may search the rest of that day and the rest of the next whole day and the next whole day after that and never find more than the few splashes of blood he saw the first day.

"Teilhard de Chardin was not talking about how to escape anguish," Mary Oliver adds, "but about how to live with it." What religion provides is a context in which the irreconcilable—our wanting to kill and hating to kill and needing to kill—becomes bearable, not erased but encompassed by a mercy larger, more generous than our nitpicking little rational minds can possibly devise. But because our pastoral religious tradition has little or no room in it for the hunt, we are left, in our culture, casting about in the toolbox of rationality, vainly searching for the wrench or screwdriver that can take the place of the shaman's voice, the voice of the raven. We won't find it. So we are left with the task of inventing our own redemption out of our own histories and confusions, finding our way, by looking back and looking around us and looking ahead, to infuse the hunt with the meaning it has always had in cultures in which it is an essential source of food.

৬

That task is not easy on either a personal or a societal level. In our culture the acquisition of food may not be even an ancillary purpose for a hunter. The people in the West who vaporize prairie dogs with high-powered .22s are not taking home any meat. Apparently the point of this sport is the great fun of seeing a small rodent explode into thin air. And here in Maine, many hunters who shoot a bear don't eat the meat. The point is not food but a bearskin on the floor. In these two examples, the role of food acquisition in the hunt has disappeared entirely, and the sole remaining motivation is "sport" in the first instance, trophy acquisition in the second.

It is hard to imagine that anyone would choose to atomize prairie dogs for any reason other than "sport," though prairie-dog gunners might like to claim that they are performing a socially useful service by ridding the plains of a so-called varmint. However, the conventional wisdom that demonizes black-tailed prairie dogs is far from wise. Horses and cattle don't break their legs in prairie-dog holes, nor are prairie dogs overrunning the western plains and consuming pasturage that should, some ranchers think, be devoted exclusively to fattening beef cows. On the contrary, habitat loss, poisoning, shooting, and disease have already reduced prairie dogs to something like 1 percent of their historic numbers. Protection, not continuing eradication, is what is urgently needed for this animal that plays a beneficial role in prairie ecology. Prairie dogs dig up the soil and help enrich it; they are a major food source for the black-footed ferret and the ferruginous hawk. So in short, the only justification for this sport its adherents can offer is the good old-fashioned fun they derive from it. If shooting droves of prairie dogs qualifies as hunting and sport, then who would ever want to be called either a hunter or a sportsman?

Motivation for hunting and fishing in the industrialized world ranges across a broad spectrum, with "pure sport," exemplified by the gratuitous killing of prairie dogs, representing one extreme and "pure utility," the other. The reasons why most people choose to hunt and fish probably fall somewhere between, with sport and meat being of varying importance from one individual to another and with any number of other factors–appreciation of nature, exercise, companionship, and change from workday routine–thrown into the mix and sometimes overshadowing both sport and meat.

In an often cited survey of hunters' motivations, Stephen R. Kellert found hunters falling into three major categories: Utilitarian/Meat Hunters (43.8 percent of those surveyed), who were primarily interested in food acquisition; Dominionistic/Sport Hunters (38.5 percent), primarily interested in "mastery, competition, shooting skill, and expressions of prowess"; and Nature Hunters (17.7 percent), primarily interested in "close contact with nature."

I suspect the responses Kellert got in his study would be unlikely to turn up in a genuine hunter-forager culture. The truly utilitarian hunter in such a culture would probably find it all but impossible to break hunting or fishing or any other food-gathering activity into a food component and a sport component or any other isolated components. He does not hunt to get close to nature because he is already in it. Of course hunting is "fun" and "sport" for such a hunter if by *fun* we mean the satisfaction that comes with deep knowledge of the natural world he inhabits and with the competence to derive a significant part of his living directly from it, no middlemen in between. Of course he enjoys hunting, just as he enjoys eating, breathing, sleeping. To ask an Inuit hunter whether he hunts for sport or for food would strike him as a bizarre question. The hunters I have come to know and respect in recent decades down here in the lower forty-eight would understand the question because they live in a culture with a fractured relationship to nature. But they, too—for themselves—would find it oddly inapplicable. Do they pick fiddleheads in spring for food or for sport? Do they tap sugar maples and make syrup for food or for sport? Take away the acquisition of food, and the exercise becomes pointless. But the practical, life-sustaining aspect of the hunting or foraging in no way lessens the deep pleasure of the activity; on the contrary.

This line of reasoning would seem to oblige me to adopt as an article of faith that I will hunt and fish only for food. If I do adopt such an article, I can then account for my perhaps excessive zeal in rescuing spiders, mice, and turtles. To kill an animal, any animal large or small, by accident or intent, and not eat it is to tear at the threads in the beautiful and intricate tapestry of nature. Killing to eat is woven into that tapestry; killing to kill is not. So the boy who shoots a songbird for the sake of killing is stricken with guilt, and the motorist who squashes a gray squirrel on the highway is filled, if not with guilt, then with a regret nearly as painful as guilt.

Fine, so I hunt and fish only for food. But how then can I catch one trout and kill it to eat when five minutes later I'll catch another one and let it go? If my purpose is food and food only, I should catch my supper and go home. I can, of course, claim I'm not killing those fish I release. I'm using heavy enough tackle that I can bring them in quickly, without exhausting them, then gently tilt the barbless hooks out of their mouths. Often I don't even touch those fish. But sometimes they're more than lip-hooked. Sometimes a tiny nymph hook is deeply embedded in tongue or jaw. I have to get hold of the fish and dig for the hook with a hemostat. By the time I realize I should have just cut the leader, the trout is on the verge of going belly-up. I hold it headfirst in the current, let it regain its strength, then watch it swim slowly and unsteadily out of my hand. Estimates of how many fish caught on flies and then released die of stress, no matter how swiftly they are brought in and how gently they are handled, range from 5 to 10 percent. (Writer-fisherman John Holt snorts at those numbers and thinks mortality can be as high as 50 to 70 percent.) The fish I've just mauled is a strong candidate for that 5 to 10 percent. If it in fact dies, I will have killed it for fun, for sport. And even if I could assume that all the fish I release would survive, how can I square catch-and-release fishing with my first principle? Maybe I'm not killing those fish, but I'm certainly catching them with total disregard for my moral imperative: hunt and fish for food only.

The catch-and-release dilemma existed, of course, long before catch-and-release became a management strategy. Size limits have always obliged fishermen to release fish. The minute I graduated into the higher realm of sport fishing for noble trout and left behind my early childhood phase of catch-kill-and-eat fishing for those ignoble warm-water perch and sunnies, at that moment I also entered the realm of catch-and-release. But not until catch-and-release was mandated on certain waters or on certain waters at certain times did we fisherfolk have to stop kidding ourselves. Before that, we could say that in the course of catching the fish we would keep and eat, we also caught and then released undersized fish. We didn't *want* to catch those fish; they were unwanted intrusions upon our mission (enjoyable) of catching some food; and in the interests of (a) preserving the resource and (b) abiding by the law, we released them. Or we may have released legal-sized keepers too, practicing de facto catch-and-release, so that we wouldn't fill our limits and thereby put a premature end to a day's fishing.

But now, on catch-and-release waters, we're really up against ourselves: If we fish those waters, we won't take home any food. We're there for fun only, for sport only. Period. We talk of playing a fish. What's play for us, however, cannot be much fun for the fish. Its behavior on the other end of the line tells me it doesn't like being there. You can find learned gentlemen who will tell you that fish don't feel pain or, if they do, they don't feel the same kind of pain that we or other mammals feel. Therefore, their pain should not be an issue. And you can find equally learned gentlemen who will tell you just the opposite. You can also find a lot of people who will tell you the whole question is a stupid one cooked up by a bunch of silly twits who just love to stew in their own moral juices. What matters is the preservation of species and habitat, they say. Catch-and-release has been demonstrably good for both. Plenty of released fish—okay, we can argue about percentages—live to reproduce and to get caught another day. Catch-and-release fly fishers are among the most avid and effective defenders of free-flowing, unpolluted rivers. A win–win arrangement if there ever was one. The fish and the entire aquatic environment benefit. Case closed.

But, alas, it is not. Ted Kerasote, hardly your antihunting and -fishing vegan, has written a thoughtful piece in which he walks all around the issue, takes in the current perspectives on it, but in the end can find no resolution. In the end he is left wading ashore on the Gros Ventre River, having just released a cutthroat trout and feeling uneasy about both the catch and the release. He has to admit he enjoys the fight, the weight and dance and struggle of the fish at the other end of his line; and he also has to admit he finds the catching and releasing abusive of the animal in a way that catching, killing, and eating is not.

The core issue that bothers Ted Kerasote and all the rest of us who have struggled with the question of catch-and-release is the issue of respect. In a true hunting culture, hunters are permitted to kill and eat animals but not toy with their lives, not treat them as playthings. As Richard Nelson observes, the Koyukon people of Alaska demonstrated their respect for animals

> *through innumerable gestures of politeness and through adherence to rules or taboos. A strict code of morality extends beyond the enclave of human society to include the entire community of life.*
>
> *In recent times, this code has also influenced Koyukon villagers' attitudes toward biological research. Studies in nearby wildlands have involved capture of small mammals, translocation of fish, and use of radio collars on caribou. In each case they felt the methods were dangerously offensive to the animals involved and likely to make them shun people or move elsewhere.*
>
> *Killing an animal for food is one thing; capturing, manipulating, and releasing it is another. As I understand it, these intrusions violate a creature's inherent right to live with dignity. Both Koyukon and Inupiaq people objected most strenuously to the use*

of radio collars, and some said they would try to kill
such an animal so it wouldn't have to go on living
that way.

In *Heart and Blood*, Nelson's solid and eminently read-
able study of the present status of deer in America, we find
examples of these same scruples in people not raised in
hunting cultures. The wildlife biologists on an Alaskan
study project who clearly feel respect for the creatures they
work with tell Nelson at the conclusion of the project that
they find it deeply troubling to have to dope the deer they
have studied, saw the antlers off the males, stuff the animals into crates, and haul them off to some other island
where the researchers hope these deer that have become
accustomed to human presence and are now an easy target for hunters will have at least a chance of recovering
their wariness and of surviving. These biologists, trained
as they are in science and in modern methods of field re-
search, nonetheless perceive these manipulations as violations of the animals' dignity. All of us who read this
passage appreciate that the study these biologists have con-
ducted and their narcotizing and handling of the animals
are in the best interest of the species and of these individual deer, but we also share with these researchers that
sense of having stepped across a line no Koyukon or Inupiaq hunter would think of crossing.

In a later chapter Nelson visits a ranch in Texas whose
owners, Bart and Debbie Gillian, not only run cattle on
their land but also manage a deer herd in a truly enlightened fashion that benefits every living thing under their

purview. They lease hunting rights on their ranch, and because they have, over the years, brought the deer population on their land into an optimum balance, the animals are healthy and the number of trophy bucks is relatively high. Because hunters at the Gillians' ranch stand a good chance of bagging a trophy animal, the Gillians can charge a significantly higher hunting fee than their neighbors who also lease hunting rights but who have not managed their deer populations as effectively and therefore tend to have large populations of small, undernourished deer. The Gillians' place would seem to be the best of all currently possible worlds; not only seem to be, it is. The animals are healthy; the vegetation is healthy because it is not overgrazed; the Gillians are healthy and making a good living because they are offering a quality product for which the market will pay a good price.

Richard Nelson, ever thoughtful and respectful, recognizes and applauds these positive aspects of the Gillians' operations, but for all that, something about the whole setup still troubles him:

> *I still felt ambivalent about the issue of wildness. As individual animals these Hill Country whitetails seemed pervasively wild, but their population as a whole was intensely controlled. Is it possible to minimize human influences on deer in such a place as this, or is it essential to manipulate their overall environment and ecology? The aesthetic and romantic parts of me believe something vital about nature had been lost here. But the realist, acknowledging that*

compromises are unavoidable nowadays, was im-
pressed by the ways Bart and Debbie Gillian had
balanced these many considerations.

We have to be realists. We have no choice. But at the same time we know that the voice we trust much more than the compromising realist's is the voice of the uncompromising romantic, and the romantic is telling us that there's something wrong in this picture, telling us that if our hubris had not brought us to where we are, there would be no need for catch-and-release fishing or for any other enlightened management regimens that nonetheless leave us feeling that something vital about nature has been lost. We all know that *wildlife management* is an oxymoron. What is wild is not managed. The Pleistocene hunter-gatherer left in all of us is at odds with our modern, managerial selves who are forced to manipulate habitats and animals for the good of both

The catch-and-release bind, then, would appear to be just one more small manifestation of our larger bind, of our having seized control of the Others, of our having made of the wild world our barnyard and playground, of having made its creatures our creatures, here to do our bidding, serve our purposes, provide us with sport and amusement. If I were true to my first principle of hunting and fishing for food only, I suppose I would declare catch-and-release fishing an unmitigated evil and advocate for its abolishment. But I will do neither of those things because I live in a world where the uncompromising romantic has to compromise with the realist; and in that world, catch-

and-release fishing meets the criteria Aldo Leopold suggested for "decent land use" but that are, I think, applicable to wildlife management as well: "A thing is right when it tends to preserve the integrity, stability, and beauty of the biotic community. It is wrong when it tends otherwise." Put quite simply, the demonstrable benefits of catch-and-release fishing outweigh any qualms I may have about it. Here, the romantic in me is ready to concede to the realist on a matter of public policy.

And where personal policy and behavior are concerned, I have to admit to hopeless inconsistency. Principle and desire are not always at one in my breast. While I rarely go fishing on waters that are strictly catch-and-release, I sometimes give in to catch-and-release fishing anyway. On "keeper" waters I may continue fishing and releasing fish after I've caught and killed the one or two fish that will make a meal. The lure of that next little eddy where a trout is sure to be feeding is just too great. I can't dismiss the scruples catch-and-release fishing inspires, but at the same time the sheer joy of the activity often overwhelms those scruples. Maybe there's a sixteen-inch brookie behind that rock; maybe I've got just the right fly for him; and maybe I'll present that fly so perfectly that the fish will strike. Fishing frenzy, in short, is often far more powerful than philosophy.

The prudent subsistence hunter practices a kind of wildlife management too, of course, because he knows if he overhunts or overtraps or overfishes he is undermining his own livelihood. But *management* seems too sterile a term for his restraint and forbearance born of natural piety. There is much more at stake for him than whether his chances to shoot a trophy buck or catch a record bass or trout improve or decline.

The prudent sport hunter supports wildlife management and obeys fish and game laws because he knows his sporting opportunities will suffer if he does not. Searching around in the toolbox of rationality and finding nothing that can take the place of the raven's voice, we make do with enlightened self-interest. I don't knock enlightened self-interest. It's got its unenlightened counterpart beat hands-down, but useful as the guidance is that it provides for the realists in us, it still leaves the aesthetic and romantic parts of us dissatisfied.

In Maine our chief bear biologist, Craig McGlaughlin, reports that current management practices, which include hunting bears with dogs and shooting them over buckets full of stale doughnuts, are maintaining the bear population at an optimum level. The population is healthy, and there are virtually no complaints about nuisance bears. McGlaughlin also notes that shooting bears over bait is a humane hunting method because the hunter gets a shot at close range and at a stationary target. There's less chance of wounding the animal. What McGlaughlin tells us about bears and bear hunting should be entirely reassuring. Wildlife management's job is to maintain healthy populations of animals, so who can object to a management regimen that accomplishes that task as humanely as possible? The realists in us can be and should be content.

But for all that, the aesthetic and romantic parts of us remain uneasy. Unable as we may be to find realistic arguments against bear baiting, we remain anxious for the bear's bitter fate and for our own souls. If Koyukon and Inupiaq people feel that a radio collar violates an animal's right to live with dignity, does it not violate a bear's dignity to shoot it with its head buried in a bucket of month-old jelly doughnuts? We are saying that the specific bear eating doughnuts in front of our tree stand is not just a representative of its species but an individual creature deserving of our respect. The realist in me can fool a lot of myself, but he can't fool my soul. That worrier. And what my soul tells me is that the bear has as good a claim to a soul as I do, that I can't act in any way toward the bear that fails to take its soul into account.

I have no way of knowing whether my soul or the bear's is immortal or whether we have the same kind of soul. My strong suspicion is that both our souls are mortal and both different. But I know that within or alongside the human, mammalian hardwiring I share with all other humans lurks an individual beast who constitutes me. And so it is with the bear or with our family cat, who is programmed to groom his fur and to sharpen his claws on any handy tree or doorjamb but is also his own unique self. If we can say to the bear, as the Abenaki hunter says to the deer, "I have killed you because I need your skin for my coat and your flesh for my food. I have nothing else to live on," then we can also ask the bear's forgiveness and hope to receive it. But if we have to say to the prairie dog, "I have killed you because I enjoy blasting you into thin air," how can we expect forgiveness? How can we dare even ask for it?

And even if we make the bogus argument that we shoot

prairie dogs to keep their numbers down, we clever human beings would still be left to wonder what business we have controlling animal populations when we cannot control our own. Because we do not make room for animal souls in our own psychic world, we do not make sufficient room for them in our physical world either. We convert their habitat to our habitat. We make corn- and wheat fields of the tallgrass prairie; we make pulpwood plantations of the northern forest. We crowd animals out of our consciousness and off their land. We can't just manage animals; we can't just attend to the well-being of their populations, with an eye primarily toward the sport they provide us, and imagine that our worrying souls will give us peace.

The paradox the hunter in the industrialized world has to deal with is that the hunt as sport—the very activity he engages in to reenter the wild world and become a compleat insider—irrevocably marks him as an outsider. Because the hunter-gatherer knows himself to be one animal among many animals that all find their sustenance in the natural world as given, he fits seamlessly into that world. By developing agriculture, we have taken the world apart and tinkered the pieces to what we thought was our own advantage. But now we find that the great advantage we have gained—our overpopulation; our conversion of habitats to our economic needs, with the concomitant extirpation of species dependent on those habitats; the ongoing and increasing impoverishment of natural systems—is turning out to be our greatest disadvantage. By domesticating a few grains—wheat, rice, corn, millet—and a few animals—pigs, sheep, cattle, horses, chickens—we were able to

massively increase food yield per acre. That increase permitted the population increases and concentrations that
have in turn accounted for the success and dominance of
agriculturally based societies. But the price of that success
has been an ever greater remoteness from the given natural world.

Which is the more successful culture after all? One in
which 2 percent of the population produces all the food for
the other 98 percent, thereby allowing the nonfarmers to
dig coal, trade on the stock market, build hydrogen bombs,
and write sonatas? Or one in which every citizen knows
and uses as many as seventy-five or a hundred edible and
medicinal plants and participates daily in the acquisition of
both plant and animal foods, one in which science consists
in the close observation of the plant and animal life that
provides human livelihood, one in which all the arts both
"fine" and "practical"–clothing, housing, music, story-
telling, drawing, painting, sculpture–are rooted in that life-
sustaining connection?

The forager's world is integrated; ours is not. For him,
subsistence, science, and art are inextricably linked together. For us, they are more often rivals to each other
rather than parts of a whole. Hunting, far from being an essential element in our household and societal economies,
comes under the heading "Recreation," subheading "Outdoor Sports," sub-subheading "Blood Sport." And within
that sub-subheading exist endless variations and permuta-
tions: big-game hunting, upland hunting, varmint hunting,
hunting with firearms, hunting with bow and arrow. And
because we have no shared cultural understanding of what

hunting is or should be, we have the endless and irresolvable debates about what is truly "sporting," what constitutes "fair chase." We keep trying to fit our jigsaw puzzle of sport, conservation, and sporting ethics together into a coherent whole, but too many of the parts we need are missing. We wind up with a picture fragmented and incomplete and a sporting community that is no community at all. *Hunter* is a term that can include everyone from the firepower yahoo who is simply out to kill something to what Stephen Kellert calls the "Nature Hunter," who knows a great deal about wildlife and wildlife habitat and is deeply conscious of the paradox inherent in killing these creatures he loves and respects. Indeed, many of the most vocal and articulate critics of hunting abuses are hunters themselves.

So if hunting in industrialized, agricultural societies is abusive and brutal at its worst and paradoxical at its best, why perpetuate it at all? The subsistence hunters—what few of them are left in this world—have no choice in the matter. They hunt or they starve. We have no such claim to necessity. The economy that feeds us has reduced hunting from a life-sustaining activity to mere sport and a sport that has spawned all too many ugly practices. So we are constantly driven back on the question of how we can possibly make peace between hunting and our worrying souls.

The hunt—and by "the hunt" I mean every form of foraging from moose hunting to clamming to berry picking—is how we acquire food supplied by nature's beneficence, not through the intermediate step of agriculture. If raising a kitchen garden and keeping a few farm animals takes us one giant step back past the supermarket and into the realm of what we think of as primary resources—the corn on the stalk, the beef on the hoof—then hunting and foraging take us one step farther into the truly primary resources, the food that existed before corn and beef were invented. By harvesting wild plants with our own hands, by taking wild meat and fish with our own hands, we are reminded—in case we have forgotten—that this primary world of soil, plant, and animal is what our secondary worlds of agriculture and industry derive from and remain dependent on.

The killing of a wild creature, freighted as it is with both celebration and regret, drives home on a personal level our debt to and responsibility toward the creature world. "I have done this myself. I have killed an animal not born and bred as food for me but an animal born to live out its own destiny. I owe it to this animal that has died to nourish me to protect its kind and to protect the world and resources that sustain it as it has sustained me." Hunting makes clear to us, on a gut-wrenching, personal level, our place in the biotic community, the complexity and beauty of that community, and so it teaches us that combination of humility, gratitude, and restraint I've previously called the subsistence hunter's natural piety.

That is the "use" of the hunt: Through the artificiality of hunting, we can find our way back through the labyrinth of artifice we live in to the reality of our first foods and to the practical knowledge and the religious understanding of the natural world that originated in dependence on those foods. To say we can find our way back is not to say, however, that we always do.

Because we humans have steered ourselves into a sorry pass, we have no choice but to steer ourselves back out. We can't just take our hands off the tiller. I have no illusions that we can restore and rehabilitate the wild and reintegrate it into our domestic lives without science and without human intervention. We have to go on living the divided, oxymoronic lives of wildlife managers, but in that process, we can choose which star we want to steer by. To whom should we look as our guides if we mean to be the "good animals" Wallace Stegner exhorts us to be, "brother to the other animals, part of the natural world and competent to belong in it"? I would look to the wild life itself and to the peoples whose foraging ways left this planet healthy and intact after many millennia. I would listen first to the Koyukon elder who said, "Every animal knows way more than you do." And down here in the lower forty-eight, I would listen to Aldo Leopold.

Leopold considered wild land and wild creatures the only valid measures of ecological health. But he also knew, as the scientist and forester he was, living on a continent already drastically altered by logging, farming, ranching, railroads, and automobiles, that we human beings had no choice but to manage, and if we were to manage well, if we were to preserve what health our lands still retained and restore to health those already diseased, then perception of "the incredible intricacies of the plant and animal community" and a "sense of husbandry" were what our place in history required of us.

Husbandry is a word closely tied to agriculture and usually suggests the application of scientific knowledge to maximize productivity in the raising of domestic crops and domestic animals. But it is clear from the contexts in which Leopold uses this term and from modifiers he adds to it–he speaks, for instance, of "wild husbandry" and "husbandry-in-the-wild"–that his understanding of husbandry takes in much more than this agricultural sense. Yet it is also clear he does not want to abandon the connection to culture and cultivation the word brings with it. If *wild husbandry* strikes us as a contradiction in terms, then the fault is with us, not with the phrase, for what Leopold is stressing is that we need to become farmers and ranchers of the wild; we need to recognize the dependence of the cultivated on the wild for vitality, health, renewal. The wild husbandman is like the scholar Leopold describes in the closing paragraph of his "Wilderness" essay: "It is only the scholar who appreciates that all history consists of successive excursions from a single starting-point, to which man returns again and again to organize yet another search for a durable scale of values. It is only the scholar who understands why the raw wilderness gives definition and meaning to the human enterprise."

But when our agro-industry set about making this continent safe for farming and ranching, it set out to exclude the wild altogether. It declared war on all nomadic hunters, both human and animal. The hunting peoples had to be eradicated first, then their animal brothers. The hunters the government hired to kill wolves were not "hunters," though they certainly had many of the skills of hunters. They were instead soldiers in the pastoralists' army, defending our sheep and cattle against the guerrilla forces of the wild. This army's first priority was to defend our domestic animals, but then, as vocal elements in the hunting community came to regard wild ungulates as their personal property, the cry went up to defend deer and elk against the wild enemy, too. We became herders of food cattle and of sport cattle.

In his younger years Aldo Leopold was not immune to that view, and not until he gunned down an old wolf did it begin to dawn on him that soldiering on behalf of the deer herd wasn't such a good idea: "We reached the old wolf in time to watch a fierce green fire dying in her eyes. I realized then, and have known ever since, that there was something new to me in those eyes—something known only to her and to the mountain. I was young then, and full of trigger-itch; I thought that because fewer wolves meant more deer, that no wolves would mean hunters' paradise. But after seeing the green fire die, I sensed that neither the wolf nor the mountain agreed with such a view."

Too much safety for the deer, Leopold saw year after year, as one state after another destroyed its wolf populations, yields too many deer; too many deer yields destruction of vegetation; too little browse yields weak, undernourished animals and eventual starvation. ". . . [T]oo much safety," Leopold concludes, "seems to yield only danger in the long run. Perhaps this is behind Thoreau's dictum: In wildness is the salvation of the world. Perhaps this is the hidden meaning in the howl of the wolf, long known among mountains, but seldom perceived among men."

Leopold misquotes Thoreau, who actually wrote, "In wildness is the preservation of the world." Thoreau probably thought there was enough world left to preserve. Leopold, writing some eighty years later, realized, consciously or unconsciously, that we were in need not of mere preservation but of salvation; that if we were to save ourselves, we had to look more attentively and diligently to the wild than we ever had before. The tame world, cleansed of the wolf and fed by agribusiness, may appear to be the safer world for us human beings, but it is ecologically the more dangerous world. The world of the forager, however, which is riskier for us personally than the farmer's world, is ecologically the safer, more stable world.

So the cultures we need to look to are the ones we have, for all practical purposes, driven off the face of the earth or at least allowed to survive only marginally and in regions that we consider marginal: the Kalahari, the Arctic and subarctic. Given the present and constantly growing world population and its nearly total dependence on agriculture, it would be absurd to propose the foraging model as one capable of realization on any but a marginal scale. But its present impracticability does not make it invalid. On the contrary, its present impracticability only underscores how dramatically we have gone wrong. If there is any vision worth pursuing, it is a vision of a world in which our human population has not grown by one-half but has been reduced by one-half–through self-regulation, let us hope, not catastrophe–one where forest and prairie have been restored to something like their original abundance and fruitfulness, and one in which many more of us could acquire at least some of our food supply through hunting and gathering.

Such a vision may well be pie in the sky now, and Leopold recognized more than fifty years ago, if not earlier, that anything like it was pie in the sky even back then. Responding in January 1946 to William Vogt's outline for a proposed Inter-American Conservation Congress, Leopold writes:

> *The only thing you have left out is whether the philosophy of industrial culture is not, in its ultimate development, irreconcilable with ecological conservation. I think it is.*
>
> *I hasten to add, however, that the term industrialism cannot be used as an absolute. Like "temperature" and "velocity" it is a question of degree. Throughout ecology, all truth is relative: a thing becomes good at one degree and ceases to be so at another.*
>
> *Industrialism might theoretically be conservative if there were an ethic limiting its application to what does not impair (a) permanence and stability of the land (b) beauty of the land. But there is no such ethic, nor likely to be.*
>
> *. . . Bill, your outline is excellent. That the situation is hopeless should not prevent us from doing our best.*

An optimistic pessimist bent on doing his best no matter what the odds, Leopold chose to advocate and practice wild husbandry. He begins his essay "Natural History" with an anecdote about two Wisconsin farmers who get up in the middle of the night to drive into the sand counties, dig up a truckload of young tamarack trees, then return home to plant these trees on their land. Wisconsin farmers had been working for nearly a century to exterminate tamarack, and in the region where these two farmers lived, they had succeeded. So why, Leopold asks, did these two farmers choose to bring back this enemy tree? "Because after twenty years they hope to reintroduce sphagnum moss under the grove, and then lady's-slippers, pitcher plants, and the other nearly extinct wildflowers of the aboriginal Wisconsin bogs. . . .

"These two farmers have learned from experience that the wholly tamed farm offers not only a slender livelihood but a constricted life. . . . Perhaps they wish for their land what we all wish for our children—not only a chance to make a living but also a chance to express and develop a rich and varied assortment of inherent capabilities, both wild and tame."

There are few people whose experience of both the wild and the tame is as deep and extensive as Leopold's was, few people who have ever brought the two together as closely and productively as he did. If there is anyone who best exemplifies Kellert's "Nature Hunter," surely that person is Leopold. Still, hardheaded visionary that he was, Leopold knew we humans born and raised in industrial societies could probably never fully reconcile our wildness and tameness. As he writes in this same essay, "We shall never achieve harmony with land, any more than we shall achieve absolute justice or liberty for people." But unattainable as he thought perfection in any of these endeavors to be, he did not abandon all hope. In the very passage where he declares industrial culture irreconcilable with ecological conservation, he also declares industrialism not an absolute; it "might theoretically be conservative if there were an ethic limiting its application. . . ." "Might" and "if." We shall never achieve harmony with land; but, theoretically, we might.

Models for how we might accomplish that grow scarcer all the time, but Leopold still found some. One was Mexico's Rio Gavilan country in 1936. In "Song of the Gavilan" he writes: "There once were men capable of inhabiting a river without disrupting the harmony of its life. They must have lived in thousands on the Gavilan. . . . Ascend any draw debouching on any canyon and you find yourself climbing little rock terraces or check dams. . . . Behind each dam is a little plot of soil that was once a field or garden, sub-irrigated by the showers which fell on the steep adjoining slopes."

Apache occupation of the region, followed by the presence of Pancho Villa's bandits, had discouraged settlement in recent times, so when Leopold went there in 1936, he found the Gavilan in the state of nearly perfect ecological health its earliest occupants had maintained there. "To the superficial eye," Leopold writes, "the Gavilan is a hard and stony land. . . . But the old terrace-builders were not deceived; they knew it by experience to be a land of milk and honey. These twisted oaks and junipers bear each year a crop of mast to be had by wildlings for the pawing. The deer, turkeys, and javelinas spend their days, like steers in a cornfield, converting this mast into succulent meat. . . .

These foods are the motive power which plants pump through that great organ called the fauna."

And the fauna of course includes us humans. "Every region has a human food symbolic of its fatness," Leopold writes; then, in a passage both serious and tongue-in-cheek, he spells out the recipe for preparing the Gavilan's specialty. "Kill a mast-fed buck," the recipe begins; it ends with: "Lay a steak on the summit of a steaming sourdough biscuit and drown both in gravy.

"The structure is symbolic. The buck lies on his mountain, and the golden gravy is the sunshine that floods his days, even unto the end.

"Food is the continuum in the Song of the Gavilan. I mean, of course, not only your food, but food for the oak which feeds the buck who feeds the cougar who dies under an oak and goes back into acorns for his erstwhile prey."

This essay, like "The Green Lagoons," which immediately precedes it in *A Sand County Almanac*, includes a strongly elegiac note. It too could close with: "Man always kills the thing he loves, and so we the pioneers have killed our wilderness." But at the same time, Leopold is celebrating the food continuum of the wild and the lives of people who found much of their nourishment in that continuum. They also raised some domesticated foods in their small terraced gardens without in any way disturbing the cycles of natural food production. The wildlings graze here like steers in a cornfield. Here, enough of an ancient hunter-gardener model remains for us to grasp what harmony with land could be and could provide: the wild meat we combine with our domesticated grain; the deer-meat steak, the sourdough biscuit, the gravy. The deer graze here like steers but are not steers. They are wildlings but also, in their wildness, an essential part of our domestic economy.

In "The Green Lagoons" the elegiac note is even stronger, stressed, as it is, at beginning and end. "It is the part of wisdom never to revisit a wilderness," the opening line reads, "for the more golden the lily, the more certain that someone has gilded it." But here too the greater part of the piece is devoted to the abundance of plant and animal life—fleets of cormorants pursuing mullet, coyotes feeding on mesquite beans—and the profusion of food that all creatures, including Leopold and his brother, Carl, found on their 1922 canoe journey in the delta of the Colorado.

"Most small game on the Delta was too abundant to hunt. At every camp we hung up enough quail for tomorrow's use. . . . All game was of incredible fatness. . . . The origin of this opulence was not far to seek. Every mesquite and every tornillo was loaded with pods. The dried-up mud flats bore an annual grass, the grain-like seeds of which could be scooped up by the cupful. . . . We could not, or at least did not, eat what the quail and deer did, but we shared their evident delight in this milk-and-honey wilderness. Their festival mood became our mood; we all reveled in a common abundance and in each other's well being. I cannot recall feeling, in settled country, a like sensitivity to the mood of the land."

For the pastoralists of the Old Testament, the desert wilderness was sorely lacking in milk and honey. It was not a good place to find food and set up domestic life. But for Carl and Aldo Leopold, hunting and foraging in the milk-and-honey wilderness of the Colorado delta, the wild and domestic fit together seamlessly. This particular wilderness provided not only an abundance of food but also an endless supply of mesquite, "the ultimate in fragrant fuels," for cooking and warmth.

"We had cooked with white-oak coals in the corn belt, we had smudged our pots with pine in the north woods, we had browned venison ribs over Arizona juniper, but we had not seen perfection until we roasted a young goose with Delta mesquite."

For someone like Leopold, who recognized the wilderness as home, it gave him all the comforts of home. As a hunter, he did not go out simply to hunt but rather to make a home in the outdoors with all that this entailed. Indeed, he felt hunting and camping to be so inextricably woven together that hunting was diminished if that domestic component was missing. And so, when he traveled to Europe in the mid-1930s, he was troubled not only by the sterility of the intensively managed German landscape but also by the impoverishment he felt hunting and fishing had undergone in Europe.

"Europeans do not camp, cook or pack in the woods for pleasure. They hunt and fish when they can afford it, but their hunting and fishing is merely hunting and fishing, staged in a setting of ready-made hunting lodges, elaborate fare, and hired beaters. . . . The test of skill is confined almost entirely to the act of killing itself. Its value as a human experience is reduced accordingly."

Leopold's two Wisconsin farmers planting their tamarack trees had an impossibly long road ahead of them if they harbored hopes of re-creating, in Wisconsin terms, the kind of wild abundance Leopold found in the Colorado delta or on the Rio Gavilan. But if they gave any thought at all to the near hopelessness of their mission, they did not let it stop them from acting on their fondest hopes, bucking a seemingly irreversible tide, and repopulating their domesticated lands with wild citizens. Nor, of course, did Leopold himself, who not only sang the praises of these two Wisconsin farmers but more than joined forces with them, too, in what he admiringly called their "utterly quixotic undertaking."

On the lands around his beloved sand county "shack," as he called it, Leopold and his family planted, in the course of ten years, more than thirty thousand trees and shrubs as well as wildflowers, ferns, and prairie plants. "On this sand farm in Wisconsin," he writes, "first worn out and then abandoned by our bigger-and-better society, we try to rebuild, with shovel and axe, what we are losing elsewhere. It is here that we seek—and find—our meat from God."

These two sentences from Leopold's 1948 foreword to *A Sand County Almanac* could stand as a credo of the hunter-gardener-farmer-forester devoted to wild husbandry. With the modest tools of shovel and ax, he tries to invite the wild back onto lands where it has been driven out, and in that endeavor he finds meat from God. Packed into the few pages of this brief foreword, we find the themes and preoccupations of Leopold's entire career, his devotion both to the wild and to the human enterprise. Disenchanted as he was with the bigger-and-better society, he never rejected his own kind but only the excesses of his own kind's blind worship of "progress." Indeed, in this foreword, as elsewhere, there are even notes of wry admiration for some of the fruits of progress: ". . . wild things, I admit, had little human value until mechanization assured us of a good breakfast." But why, Leopold implies, did mechanization not quit while it was ahead? In a sentence that echoes his 1946 letter to William Vogt, he writes: "The whole conflict thus boils down to a question of degree. We of the minority see a law of diminishing returns in progress; our opponents do not."

To say Leopold stood with one foot in the wild world and one in the tame would not be quite accurate. He stood wholly in both. "That land yields a cultural harvest is a fact long known, but latterly often forgotten." If land is not treated with love and respect for the community of soil, water, plants, and creatures it is, then the land will be degraded and impoverished, and the culture responsible will reap a harvest of degradation and impoverishment. "A culture," Auden wrote in a line that could have been Leopold's as well, "is no better than its woods."

Wild husbandry was Leopold's prescription some fifty years ago, an ongoing effort by hunters, farmers, and all the rest of us to preserve whatever of the wild we still have left and to try to restore landscape health—not to mention atmospheric and aquatic health—where the excesses of industrialism have impaired it. The hopelessness of our situation should not prevent us from doing our best.

EPILOGUE:
ASPARAGUS
REVISITED

It's late November, the last week of a deer season in which, so far, I have brought home nothing but the memory of ten white tails rapidly retreating into the woods. So quickly did those tails disappear that I could not determine whether they belonged to buck or doe. The deer, I think, are smarter this year than they were last, and I am dumber.

I know where they have been. On the hardwood slopes, I see where they have pawed the fallen leaves into turmoil in their search for acorns and beechnuts. I see where their repeated nocturnal journeys have created deer thorough-fares. At brook and ditch crossings, their nightly commuting has left the soft soil riddled with their tracks. So I know where they have been, but most of the time I don't know where they are, and when I do have a fair idea of where they might be, the thickets are too dense to penetrate without a cracking and snapping of twigs, and I am too restless to sit on stands hour after hour. White-tailed deer, I'm sure, know way more than I do.

At dusk I make my way down a hogback where I have a stand that lets me look down into two little valleys on either side. But in the hour or so I have waited there, I've been treated only to one gray squirrel's wild pursuit of another. Now, as I head home, the sun has dropped behind the hills in the southwest, and the shadows under the hemlocks are thick. Out in the open of the big hay field behind our house, there is enough daylight to see and shoot by, but out in the open there are no deer, and daylight or no, official sunset marks the end of legal hunting time.

I push across Temple Stream in the little johnboat I use as a ferry, follow the hay wagon track through the old sheep pasture and what's left of its gate, head up the slight slope toward the garden and the kitchen lights beyond.

The asparagus fronds that hover above the garden all summer in a cloud of soft green frizz are a coppery filigree now, and the millions of tiny filaments that spray out from the stalks glow with the faint light still left in the sky. Asparagus is so comically, exuberantly flamboyant when it goes to seed. "Oh, no," it says, "I'm not finished. I'm not all washed up, not by a long shot. You just watch. Come next spring, I'll be back earlier than anybody else and raring to go. You can't keep a good vegetable down." Even now, dry and sere, asparagus remains full of spirit and spunk.

And there, a bit to the right of the asparagus, is a row of leeks, some of their slender blue-green leaves still standing tall, most of them genuflecting. The indomitable kale is neither bowed nor bent. At a little distance and in this low light, the leaves arching out in all directions make these plants look like miniature palm trees, a touch of the Tropics in this northern garden where frost will soon descend.

The deer may make themselves scarce in the daytime, but at night they have no qualms about cozying up to us. The soft soil of the garden shows their footprints, large and small, buck, doe, and fawn. What was a handsome red cabbage just yesterday is today a naked stalk. The rutabaga leaves have been gnawed back to their white midribs. There is no trace of the self-propagating comfrey that grows in wild abundance along the garden fence in summer. But Temple deer are really quite considerate. They leave Rita's garden alone all summer, and it is only when the cool weather comes that they turn up in search of a few treats. Rita does not rail against these depredations. The visits of the deer strike her not as an invasion but just one more sign, like the self-renewing crops of weeds, of how the wild world wants to keep weaving itself into the fabric of our domestic lives and how, if the balance is right, the two can live happily side by side.

Fond as I am of allegory, emblem, and symbol, I can't help seeing this November as a little morality play. I divide my days between hunting and writing the final pages of this book. I'm up before dawn and out on the hill across Temple Stream at first light. By eight o'clock I'm back at my desk. By two-thirty I've found whatever words my brain is willing to relinquish today, and I go back out for the last hour and a half or so of daylight. Both the deer and anything I could call a last, conclusive word evade me.

The deer evade me because I have not made myself wild enough. I have not given myself wholly enough to them, not been patient enough, observant enough. And so it is with the last word I'm looking for but not finding. I can't call this book done and finished because, clear and urgent as the vision of a world less densely populated and restored by wild husbandry to a wilder state is to me, the path toward realization of that vision, even on a personal level, is anything but simple and clear.

I may think of hunting and fishing primarily as food-gathering activities, but the amount of food they yield in a year provides no more than occasional treats, not any staple elements of our diet. The reality of our lives is the reality of this November evening: I'm standing here empty-handed in the fading light, admiring Rita's garden, the far more important source of food in our lives in terms of both quantity and variety. Here before me, along with the promise of next year's asparagus, are the hardy vegetables we and the deer are still harvesting, and under a few patches of the white Remay we use to ward off frosts, even endive is surviving in this year's comparatively mild November. Throughout the winter months we will eat the potatoes, carrots, and beets stored in the cellar, the winter squash and cabbages stashed in a cool, dry corner upstairs, the green beans, broccoli, peas, blueberries and blackberries and strawberries in the freezer.

Agriculture is and has to be the major source of our family's food, just as it is and has to be for most human beings. And there are plenty of practical reasons why that's a good thing. I often think that if I were a better and more determined hunter than I am, I could shift the balance in our diet considerably but probably never get close to a fifty–fifty split, not even if I took advantage of Maine's six-month season on rabbits or its yearlong season on wood-chucks and porcupines. The yield from hunting could be boosted considerably by fishing, of course. Panfish–the perch, bluegills, and sunfish of my childhood–are plentiful enough to constitute a staple item. White perch abound in many of our local ponds, and just about any evening's catch will provide enough fish for two or three meals. We could eat fish for much of the year, but there is a com-pelling reason why we do not: Our fish are contaminated with mercury. Maine's Bureau of Health advises "the gen-eral population" to eat no more than two to three meals of warm-water species per month. Pregnant women, nursing mothers, women who plan to become pregnant, and chil-dren under eight years of age are advised not to eat any warm-water species and to eat no more than one meal of cold-water species per month.

That toxicological barrier to eating fish can stand as a metaphor for all the barriers that an industrial economy puts in the way of gathering and eating wild food. We have to decide how, where, when, and what we hunt and eat in light of current realities: the mercury, dioxin, and PCBs in fish; the cadmium in deer liver and kidneys; our overpop-ulation in some regions and our impacts on wildlife habi-tat and wildlife populations everywhere. If, all of a sudden, the entire population of the lower forty-eight states, let alone of China and India, decided to hunt and fish for food, we would soon not have a single wild fish or mammal left alive. Existing populations of wild creatures, even those ex-cess populations of deer that are devastating suburban Connecticut and Westchester County, could not begin to sustain the existing human population. Domestic meat animals can and do take the place of wild meat; but vegetarians argue that it is much more efficient to grow grain and feed it directly to people than to grow it, feed it to cattle and poultry, then feed the cattle and poultry to people.

Given those realities, raising animals for food seems anachronistic and hunting downright antediluvian. Why not just throw in the towel and admit that we've reached a point in history where animal husbandry is a dubious enterprise and hunting either has no place at all or ought to have none? Why not just admit that in a world where the current human population of 5.9 billion is expected to reach 8.9 billion in another fifty years, the future belongs to the bio-engineers who want to control deer and elk populations with immunocontraceptive darts and who may eventually, through genetic engineering, find a way to convert coyotes, bobcats, and cougars to strict vegetarianism? Why not teach the wolf to dwell with the lamb and the lion to eat straw like the ox?

Why not? The answer I find as I stand here by the garden fence in November's twilight is so simple it's almost embarrassing: Because the heart rebels at that dreary prospect. Because the heart yearns for the quest as much as it yearns for the hearth. Because the only true hearth is found on the quest. Aldo Leopold, arguing for public wilderness areas as "sanctuaries for the primitive arts of wilderness travel, especially canoeing and packing," goes on to write: "I suppose some will wish to debate whether it is important to keep these primitive arts alive. I shall not debate it. Either you know it in your bones, or you are very,

very old." There is ample evidence, both in this passage and elsewhere in Leopold's writings, that he included hunting and fishing in those primitive arts, appalled as he was at their corruption by the armies of motorized recreationists insisting on pushing more and more roads into our shrinking wilderness areas.

Well, I'm aging, but I'm not yet very, very old. What Leopold knew in his bones, I know in mine. I know as I stand here by Rita's garden that the partially wild world around it is as crucial to our sustenance and happiness, both personal and cultural, as the domestic foods she has so lovingly brought to fruition. We simply cannot do without the one or the other. The contribution the garden makes to our physical nourishment is much greater than that of the hunt, but its predominance does not make whatever wild food we do eat in the course of a year—whether deer, duck, trout, blueberry, or pepper root—negligible and, hence, dispensable. Every mouthful of wild food we take binds us once again to the world as *given*, not the world as shaped and engineered by humans; and the ongoing hunt for wild food takes us ever deeper into that given world upon which both our own human sustenance and everything we have shaped depends. I know of no sadder testimonial to this view than the belief of the Naskapi that the change from wild meat to the meat of domestic animals in their diet accounts for the decline of their people and the destruction of their spirit.

Intuition, the heart, the bones. We rationalistic, verbal types tend to shy away from messages coming from those quarters. One of the most sacred texts of our culture tells us, after all, that in the beginning was the Word, not the caribou or the buffalo. We mistrust knowledge we can't fit into words. We worry that if we attend too closely to what our bones tell us we will soon tumble into *Blut-und-Boden* madness, into propounding the sacred mysteries of our native soil and native blood. Probably, we think, the slaveholder felt in his heart and bones that slavery was dictated by nature, a paternalistic institution by which the superior white race raised the inferior black above jungle savagery. So many crimes have been justified by an appeal to what we have declared to be "nature's laws."

But standing here in the November twilight, I trust what my heart and bones tell me. They tell me that this garden my wife has tended with her own hands and made all the richer by her cultivation is not, like vast agribusiness enterprises and factory farms, an insult to the wild world but a welcome guest in it. The genius of the soil has been pleased with the culture she has brought to it. They tell me, too, that if I bring a similar spirit and culture to the hunt, the genius of the creature world will flourish and be pleased. The process is not a linear one, progressing ever closer to, but never attaining, Ortega's orientation point of ethical perfection. Rather, it is a circular one, the going out before dawn and returning at dusk, the trail, always new and always the same, that leads away from the hearth and back to it.

Standing here, I realize too that however attached I may be to this little valley and these hundred acres where we have lived for nearly thirty years and however much a creature of my culture I am, dependent on many of its products and services (without eyeglasses I couldn't read), devoted to many of its arts and endeavors (without books, there wouldn't be anything to read), I realize, despite all the benefits of the industrial world I enjoy, that I too, like Leopold's scholar, return again and again to a single starting point, the raw wilderness, to organize my search for a durable scale of values and to give definition and meaning to the human enterprise.

Raw in Leopold's phrase does not mean coarse or crude; *wilderness* does not mean trackless waste. The Cree of northern Quebec describe their once wild lands as their garden, the source of their food, shelter, and clothing. The raw wilderness, wherever any of it is left, is the creation still intact, not raw as in a raw wound but raw as in pure, sound, balanced, harmonious, creation as the prime source of culture, the territory and the hearthstone of the tribe. In its light, human intelligence and the works of humankind are indeed a mere bristle on the hog. In it, garden and cathedral are one, and each disappears in the other.

So for this partially wild world I live in I am grateful, but the vision that sustains me is of a world far wilder still, one in which our farms and gardens and timberlands and mines have not displaced the creation, pushing it out into the fringes of the inhabited world, but one in which the line between gardens and the wild is all but invisible, one in which the gardener is a hunter, the hunter a gardener, and both are practitioners of wild husbandry.

Here, next to Rita's garden with its promise of next year's asparagus and its fresh, abundant crop of deer tracks, that vision does not seem impossibly remote. Here, in food we raise with our own hands and with our own love and labor and in the body and blood of creatures we pursue and kill with joy, wonder, and sorrow, we find the world, our true nourishment, our sacred meal.

NOTES

PREFACE AND ACKNOWLEDGMENTS

xi-xii ". . . [O]ne of the great dreams . . ."
Quoted in Bill McKibben, *Hope, Human and Wild* (Saint Paul, MN: Hungry Mind Press, 1995), p. 219.

xiii "land yields a cultural harvest"
Aldo Leopold, "Foreword to Sand County Almanac," *A Sand County Almanac*, abbreviated hereafter as SCA (New York: Oxford University Press, 1966), p. x.

PROLOGUE: PORCUPINE STEW AND ASPARAGUS

5 In the cosmology of the Koyukon people . . .
See Richard Nelson, "Searching for the Lost Arrow: Physical and Spiritual Ecology in the Hunter's World," in *The Biophilia Hypothesis*, edited by Stephen R. Kellert and Edward O. Wilson (Washington, DC: Island Press, 1993), pp. 214–217.

6-7 On the digestive system of the porcupine, see Uldis Roze, *The North American Porcupine* (Washington, DC: Smithsonian Institution Press, 1989), pp. 44ff.

7 "a hunter of leaves . . . a hundred days afterward."
Ibid., p. 93.

8 "Every animal knows . . ."
Richard Nelson, *The Island Within* (New York: Vintage

Books, 1991), p. 26.

8 On the uses of porcupine quills and tail, see Roze, *The North American Porcupine*, pp. 3–5.

I. KID STUFF

18 "The surrounding rocks themselves . . ."
J. Fenimore Cooper, *The Last of the Mohicans*, edited and with an introduction by William Charvat, Boston: Houghton Mifflin (Cambridge, MA: Riverside Press, 1958), p. 360.

18 "Kill me if thou wilt . . ."
Ibid., p. 359.

27 "A number of anglers resent . . ."
Ray Bergman, *Trout*, 2nd edition. (New York: Alfred A. Knopf, 1952), p. 150.

II. GROWING UP CONFUSED

43 "I have precious little sympathy . . ."
John Muir, *A Thousand-Mile Walk to the Gulf*, edited by William Frederic Badè (Boston: Houghton Mifflin, 1944), p. 122.

44–45 "I have indicated . . ."

José Ortega y Gasset, *Meditations on Hunting*, translated by Howard B. Wescott, with an introduction by Paul Shepard (New York: Charles Scribner's Sons, 1972), pp. 110–111.

46 "In periods . . . which were not revolutionary . . ." Ibid., pp. 34–35.

47 This dismal practice . . .
See Barry Lopez, *Of Men and Wolves* (New York: Charles Scribner's Sons, 1978), p. 159. On status of aerial-hunt initiatives: telephone interview with Michele Keck, Anchorage office, Defenders of Wildlife, March 29, 2002.

48 "I caught this morning's . . ."
Gerard Manley Hopkins, "The Windhover," *Poems of Gerard Manley Hopkins*, 3rd edition, with an introduction by W. H. Gardner (New York and London: Oxford University Press, 1948), p. 73.

51 "The exemplary moral spirit . . ."
Ortega y Gasset, *Meditations*, pp. 101–102.

51 ". . . that in which the hunter . . ."
Ibid., p. 77.

52 the canned hunt
See, for example, Michael Winikoff, "Blowing the Lid Off Canned Hunts," *HSUS News* (summer 1994), pp. 38–43.

53 "I have killed you . . ."

Quoted in Ted Kerasote, *Blood Ties: Nature, Culture, and the Hunt* (New York: Random House, 1993), p. 1.

53 "the hint of criminal suspicion . . ."
Ortega y Gasset, *Meditations*, p. 109.

53 "Every good hunter . . ."
Ibid., p. 102.

53 ". . . the principle which inspires hunting for sport . . ."
Ibid., p. 129.

III. VENTURES IN THE STOCK MARKET

66 "Cattle raising is a relationship . . ."
Ibid., p. 137–138.

67 "Man cannot re-enter Nature . . ."
Ibid., pp. 139–140.

78 "good animals"
Wallace Stegner, "The Wilderness Letter," *The Sound of Mountain Water* (New York: E. P. Dutton, 1980), p. 147.

80 "Man cannot re-enter Nature . . ."
Ortega y Gasset, *Meditations*, pp. 139–140.

IV. DISH-FED RETAINERS

85-87 Scott and Helen were full of excellent advice . . .
Helen and Scott Nearing, *Living the Good Life: How to Live Sanely and Simply in a Troubled World* (New York: Schocken Books, 1970). See in particular chapter 2, "Our Design for Living," pp. 21–45; on not keeping animals, pp. 27–28.

94 Native American mythologies tell . . .
Anthologies of Native American legends abound with examples. See, for instance, *American Indian Myths and Legends*, selected and edited by Richard Erdoes and Alfonso Ortiz (New York: Pantheon Books, 1984).

94 The "caribou man" of the Montagnais . . .
This passage draws on Frank G. Speck, *Naskapi: The Savage Hunters of the Labrador Peninsula*, new edition (Norman: University of Oklahoma Press, 1977), pp. 80–89, especially 87–88.

96 "the mindless drabs . . ."
Paul Shepard, "On Animal Friends," in *The Biophilia Hypothesis*, p. 286.

96 "protoplasmic farrago . . ."
Ibid., p. 286.

96-97 "[Dogs'] relationship to us . . ."
Ibid., p. 287.

98 Konrad Lorenz gives lower marks . . .
See Konrad Lorenz, *Man Meets Dog*, translated by Marjorie
Kerr Wilson (New York: Penguin Books, 1964), pp. 78ff.

99 "It is a remarkable fact . . ."
Konrad Lorenz, "Part and Parcel in Animal and Human Societies," *Studies in Animal and Human Behaviour*, translated by Robert Martin (Cambridge, MA: Harvard University Press, 1971), p. 181.

100 . . . single informing idea in all his work . . .
See, for example, Paul Shepard, *Thinking Animals: Ani-
mals and the Development of Human Intelligence* (New
York: Viking Press, 1978), and *The Others: How Animals
Made Us Human* (Washington, DC: Island Press, 1996).

100 "not as stuff or friends . . ."
Shepard, "On Animal Friends," p. 278.

102 "Nothing in the forest . . ."
Mary Oliver, "A Few Words," *Blue Pastures* (New York: Har-
court Brace, 1995), p. 91.

102 "wild, valorous, amazing"
Ibid., p. 93.

102 "Humans or tigers . . ."
Ibid.

103 the "fierce green light". . .

The reference here is to Leopold, "Thinking Like a Mountain," *SCA*, p. 130.

V. CONTEXT NORTH: HUNTING ALL THE TIME

112-114 "Standing here, watching the ice come down . . ."
John Haines, *The Stars, The Snow, The Fire* (Saint Paul, MN: Graywolf Press, 1989), pp. 141–142.

115 Paul Shepard suggests *foraging*. . .
Shepard, *The Others*, p. 292.

121 "As in all living things . . ."
Bernd Heinrich, *A Year in the Maine Woods* (Reading, MA: Addison-Wesley Publishing, 1994), pp. 211–212.

124 In his 1920 book Labrador . . .
See William B. Cabot, *Labrador* (Boston: Small, Maynard, 1920), p. 341.

126 "comminglings of outer world and inner flesh"
Nelson, "Searching for the Lost Arrow," p. 205.

131-132 "corn rats"
See Richard Nelson, *Heart and Blood: Living with Deer in America* (New York: Alfred A. Knopf, 1998), pp. 298–309, on agricultural damage caused by deer in Wisconsin. On Texas game ranches, see chapter 6, "The Deer Capital of Texas," pp. 183–217.

132 "Very intensive management . . ."
Leopold, "Conservation Esthetic," *SCA*, p. 260.

132-133 On exotics and biologists' view of them, see Nelson, *Heart and Blood*, pp. 203–205. Elizabeth Cary Mungall and William J. Sheffield, *Exotics on the Range: The Texas Example* (College Station: Texas A&M University Press, 1994), presents a full picture of all the exotic species (about sixty-five) kept on Texas ranches. Burkhard Bilger's report, "A Shot in the Ark," *The New Yorker* (March 5, 2001), pp. 74–83, captures succinctly the biological, social, and ethical issues raised by ranching exotics and staging commercial hunts for them.

134 "In gaining the lovely and usable . . ."
Wallace Stegner, "Glen Canyon Submersus," *The Sound of Mountain Water*, p. 128. Stegner wrote this sentence doing his best to appreciate the virtues of Lake Powell but still finding them a sad substitute for the wonders of the canyon it had flooded out.

138-140 A Brule Sioux legend...
My retelling of this story is based on the version titled "Stone Boy" in *American Indian Myths and Legends*, pp. 15–19.

140 "This little lodge, these rocks . . ."
This speech by Stone Boy is quoted directly from ibid., p. 19.

VI. FOOD, SPORT, AND ANIMAL HUSBANDRY

143 "I think I could turn . . ."
Walt Whitman, "Song of Myself," *The Portable Walt Whitman* (New York: The Viking Press, 1945), pp. 98–99.

144 ". . . to consider Nature . . ."
Mary Oliver, "Sister Turtle," *Winter Hours: Prose, Prose Poems and Poems* (New York: Houghton Mifflin, 1999), p. 14.

146 "William, I hate fishing . . ."
Hayden Carruth, *Scrambled Eggs & Whiskey: Poems 1991–1995* (Port Townsend, WA: Copper Canyon Press, 1996), p. 80.

151 ". . . ritual allows those . . ."
Andre Dubus, "A Father's Story," *Selected Stories* (Boston: David R. Godine, Publisher, 1988), p. 461.

152 Mary Oliver quotes Teilhard . . .
Oliver, "Sister Turtle," p. 19.

152 "Teilhard de Chardin was not talking . . ."
Ibid., p. 21.

154 However, the conventional wisdom . . .
This passage draws on Christie Aschwanden, "Learning to Live with Prairie Dogs," *National Wildlife* (April–May 2001), pp. 22–29, especially pp. 26, 28.

155 In an often cited survey . . .
Stephen R. Kellert, "Attitudes and Characteristics of Hunters and Antihunters," in *Transactions of the 43rd North American Wildlife and Natural Resources Conference* (Washington, DC: Wildlife Management Institute, 1978), pp. 412–423.

157 Writer-fisherman John Holt . . .
See John Holt, "Death on the Musselshell, in *On Killing*, edited by Robert F. Jones (New York: The Lyons Press, 2001), p. 99.

158-159 Ted Kerasote . . . has written a thoughtful piece . . .
Ted Kerasote, "Catch and Deny," *Orion* (winter 1997), pp. 24–27.

159-160 "through innumerable gestures . . ."
Richard Nelson, "Searching for the Lost Arrow," pp. 216–217.

160 In *Heart and Blood*, . . .
Nelson, *Heart and Blood*, p. 88.

160-161 In a later chapter Nelson visits a ranch in Texas . . .
My summary here draws on *Heart and Blood*, pp. 185–199.

161-162 "I still felt ambivalent . . ."
Ibid., p. 190.

163 "A thing is right . . ."
Aldo Leopold, "The Land Ethic," *SCA*, p. 240.

164 In Maine our chief bear biologist . . .
See Aimee L. Curl, "Jelly Donuts Work Best," *Maine Times* cover story (May 3, 2001), pp. 4–8.

166 By developing agriculture . . .
See Jared Diamond, *Guns, Germs, and Steel: The Fates of Human Societies* (New York: W. W. Norton, 1999), in particular part 2, "The Rise and Spread of Food Production," pp. 83–193.

168 . . . what Stephen Kellert calls the "Nature Hunter" . . .
Kellert, "Attitudes and Characteristics of Hunters and Anti-hunters," pp. 414–416.

170 "good animals"
Stegner, "The Wilderness Letter," *The Sound of Mountain Water*, p. 147.

170 "brother to the other animals . . ."
Ibid.

170 "the incredible intricacies . . ." and a "sense of husbandry"
Leopold, "Conservation Esthetic," *SCA*, pp. 266, 267.

171 "wild husbandry," "husbandry-in-the-wild,"

Phrases Leopold uses, respectively, in "Conservation Esthetic," *SCA*, p. 268, and in "Wildlife in American Culture,"
SCA, p. 203.

171 "It is only the scholar . . ."
Leopold, "Wilderness," *SCA*, p. 256.

171 The hunters the government hired to kill wolves . . .
Cf. Barry Lopez, *Of Wolves and Men* (New York: Charles
Scribner's Sons, 1978), pp. 187–194. For further material on
wolf-eradication efforts and the motivations behind them,
see all of part 3: "The Beast of Waste and Desolation,"
pp. 137–199.

172 "We reached the old wolf . . ."
Leopold, "Thinking Like a Mountain," *SCA*, p. 130.

172 ". . . [T]oo much safety . . ."
Ibid., p. 133.

174 "The only thing you have left out . . ."
Quoted in Curt Meine, *Aldo Leopold: His Life and Work*
(Madison: University of Wisconsin Press, 1988), p. 478.

175 "Because after twenty years . . ."
Leopold, "Natural History," *SCA*, pp. 188–189.

175 "We shall never achieve . . ."
Ibid., p. 195.

176 "There once were men . . ."
Leopold, "Song of the Gavilan," *SCA*, p. 150.

176 Apache occupation of the region . . .
See Meine, *Aldo Leopold*, p. 367.

176-177 "To the superficial eye . . ."
Leopold, "Song of the Gavilan," *SCA*, p. 151.

177 "Every region has . . ."
Ibid., pp. 151–153.

177 "Man always kills . . ."
Leopold, "The Green Lagoons," *SCA*, p. 148.

178 "It is the part of wisdom . . ."
Ibid., p. 141.

178 "Most small game . . ."
Ibid., p. 145.

179 "the ultimate in fragrant fuels" and "We had cooked . . ."
Ibid., p. 144.

179 "Europeans do not camp, cook . . ."
This passage is from "Wilderness as a Form of Land Use," *Journal of Land and Public Utility Economics I:* 4 (October 1925), pp. 403–404, quoted in Meine, *Aldo Leopold*, p. 244.

180 "utterly quixotic undertaking"
Leopold, "Natural History," *SCA*, p. 188.

180 Leopold and his family planted . . .
Meine, *Aldo Leopold*, p. 484.

180 "On this sand farm . . ."
Leopold, "Foreword to Sand County Almanac," *SCA*, p. ix.

181 ". . . wild things, I admit . . ."
Ibid.

181 "The whole conflict . . ."
Ibid.

181 "That land yields . . ."
Ibid., p. x.

181 "A culture is no better than its woods."
W. H. Auden, *Collected Poems*, edited by Edward Mendelson (New York: Random House, 1976), p. 428.

EPILOGUE: ASPARAGUS REVISITED

188-89 "sanctuaries for the primitive arts . . ."
Leopold, "Wilderness," *SCA*, p. 248.

189 . . . the belief of the Naskapi . . .
Cf. Lopez, *Of Wolves and Men*, p. 95.